Mindscapes

This book explores the links between the psyche and the landscape—on the continuum that runs from our mental world inside to our surrounding world outside. Our sense of self is shaped by our environment, while it also helps to create the environment we perceive.

Looking to the fields of psychoanalysis, literature, art history, and neuroaesthetics—taking from both Harold Searles and Donald Winnicott, from both Emily Dickinson and Rainer Maria Rilke, from both Claude Monet and Gustav Klimt, from both Semir Zeki and V. S. Ramachandran—author Vittorio Lingiardi urges us to articulate the idea of landscape as a place that we seek all over the world, a place that serves as a psychological scaffolding for, and a reminder of, something that's already inside us. It is a discovery, but also an invention, a return-to-home. Rivers, mountains, oceans, ancient ruins, or small towns: these places inhabit our minds and our dreams, and (like psychic objects) they are embedded in our memory and our unconscious.

This book will appeal to psychoanalysts and therapists of all kinds—and to any reader who wants to understand the deep links between ourselves and our landscape in therapy and in everyday life.

Vittorio Lingiardi is a psychiatrist, psychoanalyst, and Full Professor at Sapienza University of Rome in Italy. The co-author of the prize-winning *Psychodynamic Diagnostic Manual*, he has won numerous other prizes—most recently the prestigious Sigourney Award. He has published several books and he writes regularly for the leading culture magazines in Italy.

Psychological Issues
Series Editor: David L. Wolitsky

The basic mission of *Psychological Issues* is to contribute to the further development of psychoanalysis as a science, as a respected scholarly enterprise, as a theory of human behavior, and as a therapeutic method.

Over the past 50 years, the series has focused on fundamental aspects and foundations of psychoanalytic theory and clinical practice, as well as on work in related disciplines relevant to psychoanalysis. *Psychological Issues* does not aim to represent or promote a particular point of view. The contributions cover broad and integrative topics of vital interest to all psychoanalysts as well as to colleagues in related disciplines. They cut across particular schools of thought and tackle key issues, such as the philosophical underpinnings of psychoanalysis, psychoanalytic theories of motivation, conceptions of therapeutic action, the nature of unconscious mental functioning, psychoanalysis and social issues, and reports of original empirical research relevant to psychoanalysis. The authors often take a critical stance toward theories and offer a careful theoretical analysis and conceptual clarification of the complexities of theories and their clinical implications, drawing upon relevant empirical findings from psychoanalytic research as well as from research in related fields.

Series Editor David L. Wolitzky and the Editorial Board continues to invite contributions from social/behavioral sciences such as anthropology and sociology, from biological sciences such as physiology and the various brain sciences, and from scholarly humanistic disciplines such as philosophy, law, and ethics. Volumes 1-64 in this series were published by International Universities Press. Volumes 65-69 were published by Jason Aronson. For a full list of the titles published by Routledge in this series, please visit the Routledge website: https://www.routledge.com/Psychological-Issues/book-series/PSYCHISSUES

Mindscapes

The Psyche in the Landscape

Vittorio Lingiardi

Translated by Abigail Asher

Routledge
Taylor & Francis Group

LONDON AND NEW YORK

Designed cover image: © Vittorio Lingiardi

First English edition published 2025
by Routledge
4 Park Square, Milton Park, Abingdon, Oxon, OX14 4RN

and by Routledge
605 Third Avenue, New York, NY 10158

Routledge is an imprint of the Taylor & Francis Group, an informa business

First Italian edition published by Raffaello Cortina Editore 2017
© 2017, Raffaello Cortina Editore
First English edition published by Routledge 2025

British Library Cataloguing-in-Publication Data
A catalogue record for this book is available from the British Library

Library of Congress Cataloging-in-Publication Data
Names: Lingiardi, Vittorio, 1960- author. | Asher, Abigail, translator.
Title: Mindscapes : the psyche in the landscape / Vittorio Lingiardi ;
translated by Abigail Asher.
Description: First English edition. | New York, NY : Routledge, 2025. |
Series: Psychological issues | "First Italian edition published by
Raffaello Cortina Editore 2017 © 2017, Raffaello Cortina Editore. First
English edition published by Routledge 2025." | Includes bibliographical references.
Identifiers: LCCN 2024045227 (print) | LCCN 2024045228 (ebook) |
ISBN 9781032181240 (hardback) | ISBN 9781032181257 (paperback) |
ISBN 9781003252979 (ebook)
Subjects: LCSH: Psychoanalysis. | Landscapes--Psychological aspects. |
Nature (Aesthetics)--Psychological aspects.
Classification: LCC BF175 .L543 2025 (print) | LCC BF175 (ebook) | DDC
150.19/5--dc23/eng/20250106
LC record available at https://lccn.loc.gov/2024045227
LC ebook record available at https://lccn.loc.gov/2024045228

ISBN: 978-1-032-18124-0 (hbk)
ISBN: 978-1-032-18125-7 (pbk)
ISBN: 978-1-003-25297-9 (ebk)

DOI: 10.4324/9781003252979

Typeset in Times New Roman
by SPi Technologies India Pvt Ltd (Straive)

Contents

About the author

Vittorio Lingiardi, MD, is a psychiatrist and psychoanalyst. He is a Full Professor of Dynamic Psychology at Rome's Sapienza University, where he also served as the Director of the Clinical Psychology Specialization Program in the Department of Dynamic and Clinical Psychology, and Health Studies, within the Faculty of Medicine and Psychology. He is Senior Research Fellow of the Sapienza School for Advanced Studies (SSAS). He is in charge of the Sapienza Counseling Hub for Professors and Administrative Staff. From 2020 to 2024 he was president of the Society for Psychotherapy Research—Italy Area Group (SPR—IAG).

His research interests include diagnostic assessment and treatment of personality disorders, process-outcome research in psychotherapy, and gender identity and sexual orientation. He is the author of several books and many articles published in the leading international journals of psychiatry, psychotherapy, and psychoanalysis.

He and Nancy McWilliams comprised the Steering Committee of the *Psychodynamic Diagnostic Manual* (*PDM-2*; Guilford, 2017; new edition, the *PDM-3*, forthcoming in 2025), which won the American Board & Academy of Psychoanalysis Book Prize. He is the recipient of several awards including the 2005 *Roughton Paper Award* from the American Psychoanalytic Association; the 2018 *Cesare Musatti Award* from the Italian Psychoanalytic Society; the 2020 *Research Award* from the Society for Psychoanalysis and Psychoanalytic Psychology of the American Psychological Association; the *Sigourney Award* 2023; and the *Scientific Dissemination Award* of the Italian Psychological Association.

Among his latest books are: *Body, Human* (Einaudi, 2024); *The Navel of the Dream: A Dream Journey* (Einaudi, 2023); *Archipelago N: Variations on Narcissism* (Einaudi, 2021); *At the Movies with a Psychoanalyst*

(Cortina, 2020); *I, You, We: Living with Yourself, the Other, the Others* (Utet, 2019); *Diagnosis and Destiny* (Einaudi, 2018); and *Mindscapes: The Psyche in the Landscape* (Cortina, 2017).

He is the chief editor of the series "Psychiatry, Neuroscience, Psychotherapy" for the publishing house Raffaello Cortina (Milan). He writes regularly for the newspaper *La Repubblica*, for the weekly magazine *Venerdì di Repubblica* (where he has a weekly column on cinema and psychoanalysis, called "Psycho"), and other leading cultural publications in Italy.

Author's note

Mindscapes is an idea that had been in my head for years. The starting point was a phrase from the French psychoanalyst Jean-Bertrand Pontalis: "To have any hope of being ourselves, we must contain many places within ourselves."[1] This statement pushed me to explore new territories and it also predisposed me to reflect on the aesthetic paths of our object choices and, in particular, on the role of places and landscapes in our mental life. This concept is romantic and sublime, but it's also quite ordinary and practical. I felt the need to broaden my horizons and immerse myself in what Searles, in the 1960s, called the "nonhuman environment."[2]

"Names, Things, and Cities" is a paper-and-pencil game that I played as a child and that I've loved ever since. The geographies of the land are inseparable from the geographies of the mind, and there are links between *landscapes* and *mindscapes*—links that are psychoanalytic, neuroaesthetic, and inevitably poetic. The places we love are both a discovery and an invention; we can find them because they already exist in us.

Mountains and rivers, oceans and deserts, cities, monuments, and ruins—these all inhabit our minds as psychic structures. We can see a landscape as a part of the real world, a place of personal or collective identity and memory, a mirror for our emotions, or a space for sensory immersion. *Mindscape* is a neologism that sets us somewhere in the middle, right there where we need to be: with the psyche in the landscape and the landscape in the psyche.

I tried to make the short chapters in this book as thematic as possible, but landscape is "rhizomatic," like a mass of roots—it has networks that connect any point to any other point, and that characteristic ended up taking over my writing. This means that *Mindscapes* has no specific direction or hierarchy: one can start from any chapter, one can enter and exit at will. You can read it like a panorama, letting your eye linger wherever it wishes, on whatever point speaks to you the most. I tried to keep a leash on my attraction to lists and my urge to be exhaustive, opting instead to be evocative: I hope to have found external objects capable of evoking mental states and internal objects capable of finding a correspondence in the world. Indulging my propensity for connections and for cross-disciplinarity, I let different and sometimes unrelated authors meet briefly in my pages—for example, pairing Bion with Schnitzler, pairing Meltzer with Zanzotto, and pairing Bollas with Zambrano.

Borges (the genius of libraries, dreams, and labyrinths) said he was more proud of what he had read than what he had written. I wrote this book as a *dilettante* in the Italian sense—a person who delights (*dilettare*) in the writing of it; and I hope that you, the reader, will find delight in reading it. The book is indebted to many books (for even a library is a landscape). Scattered throughout the text, all through the weave, you will find many quotations—because, as Bruce Chatwin said, a literary reference can excite us as much as a rare plant or animal. And that's not all. Recognizing oneself in a poem, in a thought—feeling them as "yours"—is an act that "reverberates," as we shall see; it is an experience that loops two people (the reader and the writer) into a shared spot. A sentence that hypnotizes us; a postcard showing *that* painting; the texture of *that* pebble; the shape of *that* shell—these are "transitional objects." They belong to us and to others, they are inside and outside, they are found and created. As for literature, it is part of a psychoanalyst's "mental diet." So let's hope that His Majesty the Satanic Jargonist of psychoanalytic jargon, will feel "eroded by eruptions of clarity," and will take offense.[3]

Scanning the shelves of books I used while writing, I can trace four key fields of knowledge that I drew upon to orient (and disorient) myself when developing this book: (a) cultural, historical, and political landscape studies; (b) poetry, fiction, and travelogues; (c) neuroaesthetics and cognitive sciences; and (d) psychoanalysis. I know the first two fields as a reader. As for (c), neuroaesthetics, I have non-experimental knowledge that I have tried to augment with insights from psychology and aesthetic philosophy. As for (d), psychoanalysis, that is my expertise, my craft—and often my state of mind as well.

Notes

1 Pontalis, Jean-Bertrand. *L'amour des commencements [Love of Beginnings]*. Paris: Gallimard, 1986.
2 Searles, Harold. *The Nonhuman Environment in Normal Development and Schizophrenia*. New York: International Universities Press, 1960.
3 Bion, Wilfred Rupert. *A Memoir of the Future: The Past Presented*. Rio de Janeiro: Imago, 1977.

Acknowledgments

I would like to thank those who listened and advised me during the writing of these chapters, helping me to keep my course and ensuring that the landscapes did not overwhelm the wayfarer: Luca Formenton, Alba Lingiardi, and Liliana Rampello. Thanks to Francesco De Bei and Guido Giovanardi for defusing my concerns and indecisions, and to Nicola Carone, Nicola Nardelli, Ginevra Protopapa, and Annalisa Tanzilli for their suggestions. Special thanks to Ginevra Bompiani for advice along the way ("I want to hear *your* voice") and to Silvia Bre (when I was writing the original Italian edition of this book) for her custom translations of every line by Emily Dickinson that I quoted. Thanks also to those who took the time to discuss specific aspects of this work with me: Mark Blechner, Fabrizio Desideri, Cinzia Di Dio, Vittorio Gallese, Aldo Gerbino, and Emanuela Mundo. But today my most heartfelt thanks goes to Abigail Asher for her magnificent translation work: thorough, patient, nurtured by our lifelong friendship.

The English translation of this book was done as part of the activities of the European Union-funded project Next Generation EU – National Recovery and Resilience Plan (Piano Nazionale Resistenza e Resilienza [PNRR]).

Evocation

It would be necessary to know how to wait, to collect—for a whole (and possibly long) life—meaning and sweetness, and then, right at the end, one could maybe write a handful of valid lines. Because verses are not, as people think, feelings (which are acquired early); they are experiences. In order to write verse, one has to see many cities, men, and things; one must know animals, one must understand the flight of birds, and one must understand the gesture with which small flowers open in the morning. One must be able to think back to itineraries across unknown regions, to unexpected encounters and long-expected departures, to childhood days that are still undeciphered, to parents we were forced to hurt when they brought us joys that we didn't understand (these were joys for someone else), to childhood illnesses that began so strangely, with so many deep and heavy transformations, to days in quiet and collected rooms, and to mornings by the sea... to the sea above all, to seas, to nights of travel that passed with a high rustle and flew up among the stars—and still it is not enough to be able to think about all this. One must have memories of many nights of love (not one night identical to any other), of the cries of childbirth and white, light sleeping mothers who are healing from the birthing. But one must also have been close to persons in the final throes, one must have been close to the dead in the room with the open window and the intermittent noises. And it is not enough to have memories. One must know how to forget them, when there are too many; and to have the great patience to wait for them to return. Because memories themselves are not yet memories. Only when they become blood in us, when they are a look and a gesture—anonymous and no longer distinguishable from ourselves—only then can it happen that in an exceptional moment the first word of a verse rises from their center and flows out.

Rainer Maria Rilke,
The Notebooks of Malte Laurids Brigge[1]

Note

1 Rilke, Rainer Maria. *I quaderni di Malte Laurids Brigge [The Notebooks of Malte Laurids Brigge]*. Italian translation. Milan: Adelphi, 1992.

Chapter 1

Human flourishing

How beautiful it is to work
in the darkness of a room
with my head on vacation
alongside a blue sea.

Sandro Penna, *Cross and Delight*[1]

Suppose a painter sees a path through a field sown
with poppies and paints it: at one end of the chain
of events is the field of poppies, at the other
a canvas with pigment disposed on its surface.

Wilfred R. Bion, *Transformations*[2]

To have any hope of being ourselves, we must contain many places within ourselves. This idea, from Jean Bertrand Pontalis, teaches us two things: one is that our history and our psyche are also a geography—we are inseparable from our places, whether this be from love or from resentment. The other is that our place is never just one place only. We need many places, he says.

I can't leave a museum or an exhibition without buying a few post-cards. I have hundreds of them. They end up in a drawer, or tucked between the pages of a book, or on a bookcase, or wedged into the corner of a picture frame (a tiny painting within a bigger one). The idea for this book was sparked when I realized that many of my postcards depicted landscapes. A cliff painted by Monet, a tempest by Turner, a lagoon by Guardi, a distant city by Cima da Conegliano, a fog by Friedrich, a watercolor by Roberts, an aquatint by Daniell, brambles by Kiefer, or

DOI: 10.4324/9781003252979-1

Burri's cracked paints. I need them. They are silent images, imprisoned between the pages of a book, perhaps, or inside a box. But I move, I travel with them inside me. And I'm continually refreshing the bond that unites landscape with paintings of the landscape—sometimes to the point of confusing the two.

How is it possible that what painters, particularly Renaissance painters, built with so little—a canvas, a piece of wood, a wall, colors—has become the very writing of our visual perception? These are *mindscapes*: landscapes gathered in the psyche and the psyche immersed in landscapes. Visual perceptions that become mental visions.

Rivers, mountains, ruins, and beaches are images "etched in our mind like psychic structures," each with "its own small universe of emotion and meaning."[3] They inhabit our memories, our travels, and our dreams. As psychic objects, they are immersed in memory. They date back to the genetic-environmental dialogue of our ancestors, and perhaps they go back to the first encounter with the face of someone who looked at us— or looked away.

The link between *landscapes* and *mindscapes* leads me to reconsider the idea of place and, in particular, the idea of an elective landscape. A place that we look for, somewhere in the world, to give shape and color to something that is already within us. It is a discovery, and also an invention, and also a rediscovery. It is a *poetic* gesture, in the Greek sense of *poiein*: to make, to generate. Indeed, in a short story titled *The Enchanted*, the Italian writer Ginevra Bompiani describes the birth of the landscape as an actual birth:

> Then she saw from that swollen belly, on which she held her hands screaming, slowly emerge between her legs a soft but firm promi-nence, and then a tender fuzz of brown hair, and then a slight pale green slope, and again a prominence, more tenuous and sprinkled here and there with dimples, small inlets, and then a spot, there a tuft or a clearing, and at the bottom, almost flush with the bed, a stream flowing minute as a vein. The belly had sagged, and the legs now lay quietly on the sheet. Between them that green and brown form, pale yet lush, lay placidly. The young man bent down in astonishment. He had never seen a newborn landscape.[4]

I look up from the page and my emotional retina, the "darkness out of which I came,"[5] presents me with the image of the *Origin of the World*, the painting by Gustave Courbet that Lacan had owned before it landed at the Musée d'Orsay.

I think of Freud who—letting his imagination run wild—read the dreamlike presence of the landscape as a way of representing female genitalia and thus the role of Mother Earth in ancient agricultural cults. I think of Jung and his studies on Demeter and Persephone as figures of psychic development, of the cycle of the seasons, of the alternation of death and rebirth. And inevitably I think of Bion, of his aesthetic conception of psychoanalysis; of his concept of "O" (as in *Origin*) in its elusive meanings;[6] of his description of an analytical encounter as a reflection of trees on the surface of a lake rippled by the wind; of the transformations in an analytical session explained as poppies that a painter transforms into pigment on the canvas.[7] The poppies are of course Monet's poppies from his 1873 painting, which scatter red dots across the field of Bion's pages. In just a few seconds, the birth of landscape has transformed in my mind into image, and then transformed into psychoanalysis.

"You can't understand who people are outside the landscape," writes Yasmina Reza. "The landscape is crucial. It's the landscape that is the true filiation. The room and the stone as much as the segment of sky."[8] We live in the landscape; her words are infinite. The landscape is environment; it is horizon, panorama, space, soil, territory: so much so that we could say that to be in the world is to recognize the landscape, to know that it is not just a backdrop—the backdrop that delimits the space of the human comedy.

Landscape is a matter for geologists and geographers, for ecologists and architects, for archaeologists and art historians, for anthropologists and jurists, for philosophers and neuroscientists. And for tourists, travelers, and explorers. In this good company, each of them creates a personal and intimate relationship with the landscape. I will try to add the gaze of a psychoanalyst to this list—as a psychoanalyst who chose to start this book with the passage from Rilke that you just saw a few pages back in the "Evocation": the most beautiful possible description of our earthly journey. As a psychoanalyst who believes in the continuity between inner and outer space, and feels that they are inseparable. As a psychoanalyst who steals from Merleau-Ponty the idea that the environment is the home for our thoughts.[9]

The degradation of the landscape troubles not only art historians such as Salvatore Settis (who calls the landscape "the great sick man of Italy") but also those of us who deal with mental health. Degradation "does not only concern the form of the landscape and the environment, and not only the pollution, the poisons, the sufferings that arise and afflict us," but it calls into question a "comprehensive decline [...] of the rules of common living"[10] and the very concept of the human being.

The Council of Europe's *European Landscape Convention*, I notice, omits the adjective "psychological" from the list of functions—"cultural, ecological, environmental, social"—performed by the landscape, in its "Preamble" defining landscape's contribution "to human well-being and consolidation of the European identity."[11] And yet our emotional orientation toward the *non-human environment* is "one of the most basically important ingredients of human psychological existence," declared psychiatrist Harold Searles when—in the 1960s—he published a study with a title that hits home: *The Nonhuman Environment in Normal Development and Schizophrenia.* Anyone who overlooks this fact does so "at peril to his psychological well-being." We are united with the non-human environment by a sense of intimate affinity, the psychological counterpart of our structural, atomic affinity with both the range of environmental elements and the evolutionary history of humankind, the "biological fate"[12] of the individual that brings us back, after death, to be part of that same environment. This conscious and unconscious link, which unites the individual to the non-human environment, is key to the development of personality—and is marked by ambivalence. The ambivalence is an oscillation between dependence and control, submission and exploitation, and it can therefore generate attitudes of respect, admiration, and protection—but also indifference and contempt. It can even reach the point of "territorial ferocity."[13]

To someone like me, who believes that the human element is always present in the landscape, even when humans are absent or invisible, the expression "non-human environment" may sound strange. For we surely agree with Simon Schama that "even the landscapes that we suppose to be most free of our culture may turn out, on closer inspection, to be its product"—no? Surely we think that "landscapes are culture before they are nature; constructs of the imagination projected onto wood and water and rock"?[14] How can we speak of a "non-human" environment, when the human itself allows us to define it as such? Searles himself, re-reading his own work on the occasion of a French translation in 1986—26 years after the first edition—answers this: "While I still consider it absolutely necessary and justified to highlight the psychological meaning of the non-human environment, I would insist that it is impossible to ever isolate this meaning from what one might call its 'human envelope.'"[15] Every environment, he continues, is a site of "shifts in mental facts relating to interpersonal relations."

The conviction that the non-human environment possesses great psychological significance emerges not only from Searles's psychiatric considerations, but also from his fortunate childhood memories: "life's meaning resided not only in my relatedness with my mother and father and sister and other persons, but in relatedness with the land itself—the verdant or autumn-tapestried or stark and snow-covered hills, the uncounted lakes, the rivers."[16] Similarly happy memories are invoked in Faruk Šehić's novel *My River*, in which Mustafa Huser, a Bosnian poet and soldier, tells of his boyhood love for his landscape, of how war destroyed this idyll and how later, devastated by trauma, he returned to seek the beauty of that lost landscape.[17]

"Here, wrapping the landscape around yourself is all that's left to do / here, turning your back"[18]: this couplet by Zanzotto seems to make a garment of the landscape. Fifty years later, the poet himself went on to erase the word "landscape" in grief at seeing it traumatized by human greed and yet still capable of giving a sense of family and identity (the passage is here below).[19] He was thus a poet who was not at all a landscapist: for him, the landscape exists not as an absolute, but only in the—consolatory or traumatic—exchange with humans.

No, you have not betrayed me, [landscape]
onto you I have
poured out all that you
(infinite absent, infinite welcoming)
cannot have: the black of the destiny/adverse or guilty cloud
of the imploding whirlpool.
You who dilute the very idea of trauma
in theater wings/silences—
indifferent and yet so relevant—
you, reluctant about the last human
cupidity of disintegration and torsion
you, maybe by now a skeleton with just a few shreds on it
but that can be brought back to life by ray of sunshine,

you continue to give me a family
with your families of colors
and hushed shadows but
moved-from-quiet shadows,
you give, you distribute with sweetness,
and with gentle distraction, the gift
of identity, of the "I," which perenni-
ally then returns, weaving
infinite self-conciliations: from you, for you, in you.

The verb *paesaggire* in Italian is a magnificent neologism: from the term for "landscape," which is "paesaggio," we get the verb *paesaggire*, which renders the idea of *walking within* (or *moving within*) *the landscape*; it focuses on "human presence and the lacerations of history" and makes the landscape a real place that is continuous with a psychic place. It is a "repository of traces," that "turf in which I had to take refuge several times, in order not to get killed during the police round-ups." Being in the landscape can lead to a "rash" on "damaged" skin, can lead to "dif-fractions" that prevent the gaze from "concentrating on a single point of history, from having a simple and clear vision."[20]

The landscape narrative moves away from the panoramic dimension and into experience. "Space extracts from us and translates things," says Rilke's poem. "For the existence of a tree to work for you, wrap around it some of the intimate space that dwells within you. Contain it on all sides. It is not delimited by itself. Only if you give it form will your renunciation become a true tree."[21] This is what it means to enter the forest, to dig into the tree, as did the artist Giuseppe Penone in his *Forest Green with Shirt*: for him, a leader of the "Arte Povera" movement, breath is sculpture and a fingerprint is a pictorial image.

Our relationship with the landscape does not culminate with our gaze and our contemplation. It involves the body and its sensory participa-tion; it is charged with affection and memory and it becomes an element of identity.

An operational definition of "landscape" (even urban landscape) cannot disregard beauty, but it cannot limit itself to beauty alone; it must shift from landscape as an "aesthetic" object (to be looked at) to landscape as an "ethical" fact: a landscape to be lived in, linked to the health, happiness, and well-being of individuals and communities, to economic balance and productivity.[22]

Ko au te awa, ko te awa ko au ("I am the river, the river is me") is the Maori saying that celebrates the Whanganui River in northern New Zealand. That river is now recognized as a legal entity—after a legal battle that lasted 170 years—and is represented by a member of the Maori community and by a member of New Zealand's government. For the first time ever, a river has the legal status of a living being, whose "health and well-being" must be guaranteed.

According to the *European Convention*, landscape is a part of territory "whose character is the result of the action and interaction of natural and/or human factors." The signatory states undertake to recognize it legally "as an essential component of people's surroundings, an expression of the diversity of their shared cultural and natural heritage, and a *foundation of their identity*."[23] Landscape, woven as it is into historical and artistic heritage, is therefore a "theater of democracy," says Settis.[24] In my view, this applies to language too. I consider that our natural heritage also includes the dark forest where Dante finds himself at the start of the *Inferno*, as well as that part of Lake Como where Manzoni begins *The Betrothed*, and so many other places. For this reason, I'm dismayed when I see the landscape get wrecked, but also when I see it manipulated for commercial and advertising purposes: the leap from landscape *as an artistic invention* to landscape *as an advertising invention*. For example, the leap when landscape gets used as a screensaver, with those Photoshopped mountains, bleached-out beaches, electric-blue sea, and tidily combed deserts. A leap from one person's paintbrush to absolutely everybody's computer.

"Who can forget those moments when something that seems inanimate turns out to be vitally, even dangerously, alive?" So begins *The Great Derangement* by Amitav Ghosh,[25] a book that honors the life and vitality of nature and its landscapes—landscapes that we mistreat and then claim to respect by putting them on display, on our computer screen or our phone screen, or idealizing them on the glossy pages of some travel-agency advertisement or poster. Reading his thoughts, reading his "rebukes" to a humanity that seems to regard the landscape as if it were a spectacle staged for its own delight, I was struck by how radical is his non-anthropocentric stance, and by his regret over lost ancestral memory. In a kind of "political animism," Ghosh recounts a pre-industrial, pre-capitalist era when we "knew" that cyclones had real eyes; when rivers carved the earth with their own artistic sensibilities; when plants grew in non-random directions. Ghosh's ancestors knew that all these natural elements are alive in themselves and in their own way—that they certainly do not exist *for* us. The idea that the non-human environment teems with subjects that have "intention," that nature is not an inanimate collection of objects for our consumption: this idea can tie in, nowadays, to some psychoanalytic thinking (in the work of Randall,[26] for example, and Keene[27]) on how we relate to nature, and on our omnipotent fantasy that nature is an inexhaustible resource at our disposal. Ghosh's position, however, is more radical than the conclusions that we—the psychoanalysts who are interested in the human-to-environment relationship—reach when we try to interpret the wicked exploitation of the last century (and much farther back, even, if we consider colonial predations). Many of the proposed psychological explanations, in fact, imply the idea of a "personified" nature as a patient, mute, martyred entity that accommodates our projections, swallows our waste, and shoulders the burden of our insatiable demands for nourishment and compassion; or a vindictive and susceptible authority, from which exemplary retaliation is to be expected, sooner or later. In either case, nature is once again flattened in an anthropocentric way: it gets shoved back into the role of *Mother Nature*. In Ghosh's writings, instead, nature once again becomes independent and alive, more natural than supernatural: a set of "subjectivities" that express themselves, peacefully or violently, regardless of how any human imagination might use them. In describing the dynamics of reification, control, and possession of the natural environment, Ghosh shows us a human being who is not trained in respect—who is practically bewildered by otherness. A human being who (perhaps because he is governed by fear) is incapable of grasping the "other-than-self" as an "other-complete-unto-itself."

A century ago, Matisse complained that everything we see is deformed by habits and by the accumulation of already-prepared images. These images (he said) are to perception as prejudice is to intelligence: getting rid of them requires a certain amount of courage. Even a superficial relationship with images—the bulimic gobbling-up of images, stripping them of meaning, the touristic falsification of images, the uncritical broadcasting or (even worse) violent broadcasting of images—can be considered forms of iconoclasm: the destruction of the image and its sacredness. But images should be rescued, lifted out of the marketplace of trivialization and placed back at the heart of psychic experience.

In this sense, this book is also meant as a domestic attempt at imaginal care and landscape safekeeping.

Even though landscape-art, tourism, and exoticism have accustomed us to the pairing of landscape and beauty—a beauty that is often false, that leaves an "awful taste of simulacrum"[28]—*beauty* is not the subject of this book. The psyche encounters landscape in all sorts of places: places sublime or domestic, neglected or cared-for, burned or marred by overbuilding, or left fallow.

In a book titled *Reflected Perception* (*La percezione riflessa*), Fabrizio Desideri brings a philosopher's challenge to the idea that "aesthetic facts are comparable to facts of an emotional and/or psychological nature" and the idea of "the reducibility of aesthetic judgments to cognitive judgments."[29] In a word, he opposes the reduction of aesthetics to psychology. Quoting him here allows me to clarify that I won't be philosophizing when I speak of "beauty" in these pages—for example, with regard to the "aesthetic conflict" that Meltzer cites when he remarks that the newborn child is sensitive to the beauty of the mother, which is the beauty of the world: overwhelming, fragile, enigmatic. If I call attention to the "beauty" of a landscape here, it will not be because that landscape is "beautiful," but because its aesthetic impact—whatever it is—will ignite a neural circuit that can produce a psychic event.

For Meltzer, the encounter with maternal beauty triggers a storm in the child, which I imagine as waves that bring delight and torment because they drag along with them—as in a whirlpool of foam and stones—experiences that are hard to reconcile, such as fusion and separateness, intimacy and enigma. Depending on how we navigate this storm, we may someday be able to enjoy a beauty that is not only "the beginning of terror"[30]—indeed, the root of the word suggests goodness (the Latin *bellus*, "beautiful," is diminutive of an ancient form of *bonus*, "good").

What interests me about Desideri's observations is the way he positions the exploration of the environment with the *aesthetic genesis of subjectivity* rather than with a *subjective genesis of the aesthetic*. Aesthetic feeling, he declares, is in fact "expressive of a harmonious idea of the relationship between corporeality and aspects/objects of the world"[31] and—from a springboard of emotional experiences—contributes to the formation of our subjectivity. It is inevitable that the positive and negative characteristics of the Self–Other relationship, and of its regulation, indelibly inform one's perceptual experience as well as one's relationship with objects and one's exchanges with the world.

The world of objects, the way we choose them and use them, is an "extraordinary vocabulary" that allows us to express the aesthetics of our Self. Objects, environments, and landscapes have specific evocative effects that help to form our internal world and generally "the eros of form in being."[32] They operate in six ways at least, Bollas says: sensory, structural, conceptual, symbolic, projective, and mnestic (related to memory). Thus the "external" object that evokes mental states is evocative, as is the "internal" object that we continue to seek throughout the world.

I felt joy when I discovered concordant thoughts in one of the poet Zanzotto's writings titled "Il paesaggio come eros della terra" (The landscape as the eros of the earth) which describes landscape as an "inextricable tangle of phantasms that adhere to individual experience" that "bursts into the human soul from early childhood," producing an "initial amazement" that gives rise to the child's "interminable series of attempts (tactile, gestural, visual, olfactory, phonatory...) to come to experience things as they occur." The poet's idea is that our development is marked by a continuous exchange with the landscape as a *total perceptive horizon*. This is a process that takes place "within the self, within the brain," but that is set "within the landscape, a horizon within a horizon: a psychic horizon (established by the perceptible landscape) within a landscape horizon (encompassing, always exceeding, always 'beyond' the actual potential of human experience)."[33]

Another great poet, Pasolini, uses the splendid regional dialect of his native Friuli to render the pattern of landscape, subjectivity, and "eros in the form of being": "O young me! I am born / in the smell that the rain / sighs out from the meadows / of living grass... I am born / in the shimmer of the irrigation ditch."[34] We see this thread again running through Pasolini's later poem, in a distant part of Italy, in the landscape of the working-class quarters of Rome:

> I come from the ruins, from the churches,
> from the altarpieces, from the abandoned villages
> in the Apennines or the Alpine foothills,
> where the brothers lived.
> I walk along the Tuscolana road like a madman,
> along the Appian Way like a dog without a master.

Or I watch the twilight, the mornings
over Rome, over the Ciociaria, over the world,
like the first acts of Post-History,
which I witness, by privilege of birth,
from the extreme edge of some
buried age.[35]

A circular link is created between the *aesthesic* (perceptual) experience and the *aesthetic* experience—between cognitive discrimination and emotional resonance. The presence, or the absence, or the intermittence of the person who raised us will be crucial in the encounter with objects and therefore in the formation of subjectivity. The aspects/objects of the world will enter into the *mindscape*, shaping it and being shaped by it. The *aesthetic attunement* with the world takes shape in the relational climate that is created around the child's perceptual experiences: that's what our tastes and dislikes will depend on. One can therefore hypothesize that the infant's aesthetic experience is decisive not only for the future definition of his or her identity, but also in allowing his or her *human flourishing*.[36]

These reflections on aesthetics and psychoanalysis make me think about the circular three-part interaction—among child and caregiver and environment—in light of that primacy of experience that Dewey defined as "heightened vitality," and "active and alert commerce with the world." This definition led him to link artistic production to the "continuity of esthetic experience with normal processes of living." As this philosopher, psychologist, and pedagogue of liberal ideas wrote in 1934:

life goes on in an environment; not merely *in* it, but because of it, through interaction with it. No creature lives merely under its skin; its subcutaneous organs are means of connection with what lies beyond its bodily frame, and to which, in order to live, it must adjust itself, by accommodation and defense but also by conquest.

[...] How is it that our everyday enjoyment of scenes and situations develops into the peculiar satisfaction that attends the experience which is emphatically esthetic?[37]

Dewey's observations seem to anticipate (as we'll see in later chapters) some aspects of the contemporary neuroaesthetics advocated by Semir

Zeki, who dismisses the reductive model of vision (just retinal visual perception with brain decoding) and proposes a far more complex mechanism of vision, a mechanism that is active and that branches out into different brain areas.

Returning to the intertwining of the genesis of subjectivity with care-giving and the formation of the *mindscape*, I think of Daniel Stern's hypothesis that change is based on lived experience—even simply look-ing into the eyes of someone who is looking at us, or taking a breath while talking to someone. Stern dedicated a whole book to the impor-tance of the "present moment" (in all relationships: with a mother, a father, a partner, a therapist). That book, *The Present Moment in Psychotherapy and in Daily Life*, arrived at its final title by traveling along an interesting path. The early provisional version was *A World in a Grain of Sand*, from William Blake's poem. The second title was *The Dark Side of the Moon*. Then came *The Moment of Encounter*. This series of titles clearly reflects Stern's desire to highlight different aspects of his thought: the attention to microprocessual dynamics; then the dark side of intersubjectivity; then co-creativity and the foundation of an intersubjective consciousness, with an eye to what he called the devel-opment of a "vital affection" and a therapeutic encounter understood as a "shared affective journey."

Looking at this progression, with landscape in mind, Stern's titles— the grain of sand, the face of the moon, the sharing of a journey—seem to *situate* the path of psychoanalysis (as therapy and as theory) in a landscape, fostering a model that is both perceptive and visual. Not only the psyche in the landscape, but also psychoanalysis in the landscape. So it is not surprising to read that, for Stern, an "affective conditional jour-ney" is when

> two people traverse together a feeling-*landscape* [...]. During this several-second journey, the participants ride the crest of the present instant as it crosses the span of the present moment, from its horizon of the past to its horizon of the future [...] they pass through an emo-tional narrative *landscape* with its *hills* and *valleys* of vitality affects, along its *river* of intentionality (which runs throughout), and over its peak of dramatic crisis. It is a voyage taken as the present unfolds. A passing subjective landscape is created and makes up a world in a grain of sand.[38]

In a book that I produced with Gherardo Amadei and other colleagues, Amadei showed his typical creative sensibility in titling his essay, "A '*Lonely Planet* Guidebook' for the Relational Clinician," once again setting psychoanalysis in a place and in a territory. What would be the hypothetical "cover photo" that he pictures for his *Lonely Planet* guidebook, which—in a bit of wordplay—he transforms into a *Lovely Planet*?

A high, wide valley, whose walls, rich in views, gently slope down to an imposing river that flows rich in water, running nearly straight towards the ocean: not an idealized arcadia, but nature captured in its *wilderness*, that is welcoming but also imposes respect for the beauty of the uncontaminated. This could be a description, inevitably imperfect, of a painting by Thomas Cole, one of the leaders of the Hudson River School, the first school of painting to be considered genuinely American in origin. His sensitivity towards nature was akin to that of modern ecology [...].[39]

So, a psychic landscape is reflected in an ecological tradition that is in turn reflected in a philosophical and artistic tradition: in John Dewey and George Herbert Mead, Henry David Thoreau and Walt Whitman.

I thought I had invented the word *mindscape*, but actually mindscape is a neologism that boasts millions of hits on Google and is even the title of a film. I chose it as the title of this book from among numerous possibilities because, by evoking the relationship between psyche and landscape, it places us in between the two, where we need to be. With the psyche in the landscape and the landscape in the psyche.

We are happily in the landscape when we experience a correspondence between what we see and what we feel. A *harmony* between what is around us and what we feel in us. Like the "sea-gaze" described by Elvio Fachinelli: "The 'I' as a gaze that learns not a landscape, or several landscapes, but learns itself as a landscape."[40]

Our landscapes have become our landscapes because we recognized them the moment we found them. They are the result of the encounter between what we see (the *panorama*, which comes from the Greek terms for "everything I see") and our aesthetics of objects, our memory and our solitude.

Notes

1 Penna, Sandro. "Croce e delizia [Cross and Delight]," Italian translation in *Poesie*. Milan: Garzanti, 1997.
2 Bion, Wilfred Rupert. *Transformations*. London: Routledge, 1965, p. 1. Copyright © 2014 by The Estate of W. R. Bion.
3 Bollas, Christopher. *Being a Character: Psychoanalysis and Self-Experience*. New York: Hill and Wang, London: Routledge, 1992.
4 Bompiani, Ginevra. *L'incantato [The Enchanted]*. Milan: Garzanti, 1987, pp. 21–22.
5 Rilke, Rainer Maria. *Libro d'ore [The Book of Hours]*. Italian translation in *Poesie (1895–1908)*, Vol. 1. Turin: Einaudi-Gallimard, 1994.
6 We can paint the O as simultaneously "origin," a zero, a vagina, darkness, a thing in itself; real, infinite void; terror. It is, says Civitarese ("Bion and the sublime: The origins of an aesthetic paradigm"), one of the most elusive Bionian concepts, from which the subject can obtain knowledge and thought, but from which it can also be devoured. Bion (*Transformations*, 151), quoting Milton, likens the O to the "void, formless and infinite" with which the child comes into the world. Grotstein (*A Beam of Intense Darkness*) believes that we can never know the real O; that we can know only its derivatives, which are liars. Yes, because in order to be "tolerated," the O must undergo a transformation into a lie. Knowing the ultimate reality of one of our emotions—anguish, fear—or of one of our ways of being, is almost impossible. We can only deal with attenuated forms, "lies," of the real O—maybe in a dream, in the course of a creative experience or of an analytic session, or in an encounter with a significant person. Any truth, in order to be experienced and shared, must have areas of lies around it, as Bion and Grotstein would say. Without a lie as a "handle," writes Ferro (*Pensieri di uno psicoanalista irriverente [Thoughts from an Irreverent Psychoanalyst]*), "truth [...] would resemble a frying pan that someone asked us to pick up, while potatoes are being fried in the pan in steaming oil, at an unapproachable temperature: we need the lie-handle in order to be able to hold the pan and the truth (as well as the excellent fried potatoes that the truth gives us)."
7 All of these images are from Bion, Wilfred Rupert. *Transformations*. London: Routledge, 1965.
8 Reza, Yasmina. *Babylon*. Translated by Linda Asher. New York: Seven Stories Press, 2018.
9 Merleau-Ponty, Maurice. *Phenomenology of Perception*. Translated by Donald A. Landes. New York: Routledge, 2013.
10 Settis, Salvatore. *Paesaggio, Costituzione, Cemento. La battaglia per l'ambiente contro il degrado civile [Landscape, Constitution, Concrete: The Battle for the Environment against Civil Degradation]*. Turin: Einaudi, 2010, p. 283.
11 *Council of Europe Landscape Convention (ETS No. 176)*, www.coe.int/en/web/conventions/full-list?module=treaty-detail&treatynum=176, 1.

12 Searles, Harold. *The Nonhuman Environment in Normal Development and Schizophrenia*. New York: International Universities Press, 1960. (French translation: *L'environnement non humain*. Paris: Gallimard, 1986), pp. 6 and 4.

13 Steiner, George. *The Idea of Europe*. London: Nexus Institute, 2004.

14 Schama, Simon. *Landscape and Memory*. New York: Vintage Books, 1995, pp. 9 and 61.

15 Searles, Harold. *The Nonhuman Environment in Normal Development and Schizophrenia*. New York: International Universities Press, 1960. (French translation: *L'environnement non humain*. Paris: Gallimard, 1986), pp. xxvii and xxxi.

16 Searles, Harold. *The Nonhuman Environment in Normal Development and Schizophrenia*. New York: International Universities Press, 1960. (French translation: *L'environnement non humain*. Paris: Gallimard, 1986), p. ix.

17 Šehić, Faruk. *Quiet Flows the Una*. Newcastle: Istros Books, 2016, p. 61.

18 Zanzotto, Andrea. *Ormai [By Now]*. In *Dietro il paesaggio [Behind the Landscape]*. Milan: Mondadori, 1951. Copyright The Estate of Andrea Zanzotto. Published by arrangement with The Italian Literary Agency.

19 Zanzotto, Andrea. *Ligonàs [Ligonàs]*. In *Sovrimpressioni [Superimpressions]*. Milan: Mondadori, 2001, p. 839. Copyright The Estate of Andrea Zanzotto. Published by arrangement with The Italian Literary Agency.

20 Andrea Zanzotto, quoted in Paolini ("Colloquio con Andrea Zanzotto. Confusioni e distinzioni ["Interview with Andrea Zanzotto. Confusions and Distinctions"], 106). *Diffrazioni, eritemi [Diffractions, Erythemas]* is the title of a poem contained in *Galateo in bosco [The Woodland Book of Manners]*. See also Zanzotto, Andrea. *Poesie e prose scelte*. Milan: Mondadori, 1999, p. 1254.

21 Rilke, Rainer Maria. *Poesie sparse [Scattered Poems] (n. 98)*, Italian translation in *Poesie [Poems] (1908–1926)*, Vol. 2. Turin: Einaudi, 1995, p. 291.

22 Settis, Salvatore. *Cieli d'Europa. Cultura, creatività, uguaglianza [The Skies of Europe. Culture, Creativity and Equality]*. Turin: UTET, 2017, pp. 95–96.

23 The italics are mine. The European Landscape Convention aims to promote the protection, management, and planning of European landscapes and to foster European cooperation. It was adopted by the Committee of Ministers of the Council of Europe in Strasbourg on July 19, 2000, made available for signing by the member states of the organization in Florence on October 20, 2000, and implemented by the Italian State with a special law in 2006.

24 Settis, Salvatore. *Architettura e democrazia. Paesaggio, città, diritti civili [Architecture and Democracy – Landscape, Cities, Civil Rights]*. Turin: Einaudi, 2017.

25 Ghosh, Amitav. *The Great Derangement: Climate Change and the Unthinkable*. Chicago: University of Chicago Press, 2016, p. 3.

26 Randall, Rosemary. "Loss and Climate Change: The Cost of Parallel Narratives," *Ecopsychology* 1, no. 3 (2015), pp. 118–129.

27 Keene, John. "Unconscious obstacles to caring for the planet: Facing up to human nature," in *Engaging with Climate Change: Psychoanalytic and Interdisciplinary Perspectives*, edited by Sally Weintrobe. Routledge, 2012, pp. 144–159.

28 Osborne, Lawrence. *The Naked Tourist*. New York: North Point Press, 2006, p. 3.

29 Desideri, Fabrizio. *La percezione riflessa. Estetica e filosofia della mente [The Reflected Perception. Aesthetics and Philosophy of Mind]*. Milan: Raffaello Cortina, 2011, p. xvi.

30 Rilke, Rainer Maria. *Prima elegia duinese [First Duino Elegy]*. Italian translation in *Poesie [Poems]* (1908–1926), Vol. 2. Turin: Einaudi-Gallimard, 1995, p. 55.

31 Desideri, Fabrizio. *La percezione riflessa. Estetica e filosofia della mente [Reflected Perception. Aesthetics and Philosophy of Mind]*. Milan: Raffaello Cortina, 2011.

32 Bollas, Christopher. *Being a Character: Psychoanalysis and Self-Experience*. New York: Hill and Wang. London: Routledge. 1992.

33 Zanzotto, Andrea, "Il paesaggio come eros della terra [Landscape as Eros of the Earth]," in *Luoghi e paesaggi [Places and Landscapes]*. Milan: Bompiani, 2013, pp. 29–38. Copyright The Estate of Andrea Zanzotto. Published by arrangement with The Italian Literary Agency.

34 Pasolini, Pier Paolo. "O me donzel," in *Poesie a Casarsa [Poems to Casarsa]*, © Garzanti S.r.l., Milan, Gruppo editoriale Mauri Spagnol. The lines in dialect are: "O me donzel! Jo i nas / ta l'odòur che la ploja / a suspira tai pras / di erba viva… I nas / tal spieli da la roja."

35 Pasolini, Pier Paolo, "La realtà [Reality]." In *Poesia in Forma di Rosa [Poetry in the Form of a Rose]*; © Garzanti Editore s.p.a., 1964, 1976; © 1999, 2001, Garzanti S.r.l., Milan.

36 British philosopher Elizabeth Ascombe was the first to propose that the Aristotelian concept of *eudaimonia* could be translated as "human flourishing."

37 Dewey, John. *Art as Experience*. New York: Perigee, 1984, pp. 19, 10, 13, and 12.

38 Stern, Daniel. *The Present Moment in Psychotherapy and Everyday Life*. New York: Norton, 2004, p. 172; italics added.

39 Amadei, Gherardo. "Una *Lonely Planet* per il clinico relazionale [A 'Lonely Planet Guidebook' for the Relational Clinician]," in *La svolta relazionale. Itinerari italiani [The Relational Breakthrough. Italian Itineraries]*, edited by Vittorio Lingiardi, Gherardo Amadei, Giorgio Caviglia, Francesco De Bei. Milan: Raffaello Cortina, 2011, p. 33.

40 Fachinelli, Elvio. *La mente estatica [The Ecstatic Mind]*. Milan: Adelphi, 1989, p. 19.

Chapter 2

Psychoanalytic spaces

We are born [...] provisionally, it doesn't matter where. It is only gradually that we compose within ourselves our true place of origin so that we may be born there retrospectively and each day more definitely.

Rainer Maria Rilke, *Milanese Letters*[1]

For a long time, I have been playing with the idea of structuring the space of life—bios—graphically on a map.

Walter Benjamin, *Berlin Chronicle*[2]

Hillman reproached psychoanalysis for having neglected the souls of locations; he invited us to throw open the windows of the analysis room. And he was right: those windows had stayed shut for too long, thus saturating that claustrophilic area, hidden in the analytical relationship. And yet Freud had used a train trip as the model for his theory of free association: "Act as though [...] you were a traveller sitting next to the window of a railway carriage and describing to someone inside the carriage the changing views which you see outside."[3] And "traversal" is the term Pontalis uses to describe the experience of analysis; he prefers it to the more usual term, "process."[4] After all, as Bruce Chatwin used to say, isn't an uncharted landscape a good reason to plan a trip?[5]

Even when it's sealed up in a closed room, psychoanalysis is immersed in space and landscape: just think of Winnicott's *ambient mother*, Searles' *non-human environment*, Kahn's *fallow field* (as a silent condition; transitional, seemingly unproductive, but creative), and Bromberg's *standing in the spaces*—to name a few. In the offices of Jungian analysts

DOI: 10.4324/9781003252979-2

who practice sandplay therapy (a clinical technique developed by Dora Kalff in the 1950s), landscapes of the psyche appear, *mindscapes* constructed by the patient with his own hands using sand, water, and small objects provided by the analyst. Playing with sand has proved to be helpful to people uprooted from themselves or from the world, for seriously unwell psychiatric patients, for victims of abuse and torture, and for migrants fleeing war and terror.

The analytical story, writes Ferro in the wake of work by Madeleine and Willy Baranger, takes place in a *bipersonal field*, a terrain of encounter between the characters that inhabit the inner worlds of the patient and of the analyst, a landscape where the analyst can observe both himself and the analysand. In the field, the analytic situation has its own spatio-temporal structure; is oriented along specific lines of force and development; and possesses both general objectives and momentary objectives. The field can therefore be considered the analytic space, a variable terrain, marked by emotions and proto-emotions that belong to the analytic pair and that are continuously transformed into narratives.

It is no coincidence that, in order to give us an image of the analytical field, Ferro resorts to the fantastic cartography of the *Poem of the Lunatics* (*Poema dei lunatici*) by Ermanno Cavazzoni, on which Fellini based his film *The Voice of the Moon* (*La voce della luna*). Ferro describes Cavazzoni's imaginary water map as a place where "the borders of the regions undulate, as happens in reality."[6] Cavazzoni envisioned the printer's ink fragmenting as currents moved across the map—like clouds shredding in the wind, like the fog in a valley blotting all borders and the outlines of mountains and meadows.[7] Thus the field coincides with its narration which—at the moment of completion—is already elsewhere.

Psychoanalysis itself, "put to the test by the redefinition of its own boundaries," becomes a "continuously updated map" that can trace "places to come."[8] This is the exact opposite of the reassuring maps, fixed and mendacious, that Wisława Szymborska jokes about in her poem, "Map": peaceful maps that we can spread out on the table, with verdant valleys, friendly blue oceans, volcanoes that do not explode—above all, maps without mass graves nor aggressive peoples. These are maps that the poet loves because they tell her lies as they sketch a world of peace, a world other than our own.[9]

Open space is the term Louis Sander chooses to refer to those precocious moments of "optimal disengagement" between child and parent in which the infant can explore himself and his surroundings. It's an activity, says Jessica Benjamin, that "one baby's parents aptly called 'doing Tai Chi.'"[10] An early possibility of building one's own *open space* seems to me to be the basis of any future ability to be alone (even in the presence of the other)[11] and immersed in the landscape. It is in these rare moments, when we don't feel compelled to respond to internal and external stimuli, that our mind can wander and we can develop a special kind of creative and authentic attunement with ourselves and the environment. It's an experience that links back to when we first learned to transfer our curiosity from the maternal body to the outside world, which began to take shape as a separate world but was also part of us and of those who cared for us and nurtured us. Just as an infant's mother absorbs and processes her baby's emotions (what Bion calls "reverie"), landscape too can serve in this way, becoming a *mindscape*. The landscape can help us do what Bion—evoking Keats' *negative capability*—teaches analysts to do: to suspend desire and memory, to tolerate uncertainty, mystery, and doubt, and to welcome thoughts as they fluctuate. Learning Emily Dickinson's lesson: "The revery alone will do:"

> To make a prairie it takes a clover and one bee,
> One clover, and a bee.
> And revery.
> The revery alone will do,
> If bees are few.[12]

The moment of an *open space* is also the moment when the child is potentially most receptive, curious, and attentive to the environment. His or her early transitional experiences form a continuum with the more evolved capacity for contemplation, for creation, and for discovery of the outside world and its objects. At some point, says Winnicott, the mother will—perhaps unconsciously—produce "a situation that may with luck result in the first tie the infant makes with an external object," in the sense of "an object that is external to the self from the infant's point of view."[13] We might imagine the child's experience, Benjamin suggests, as something like this: "'Reality recognizes me so I recognize it—wholly, with faith and trust, with no grudge or self-constraint.' Thus the transitional realm allows 'the enjoyment and love of reality,' and not merely adaptation to it."[14]

Some time ago I received this email from a friend:

Dear Vittorio, I am writing in a moment of peace after a bad night with Anton, who had a cold and was frightened, and had eyes full of tears—now he is asleep. What can I say? After various vicissitudes, at four AM we were both wrapped in blankets amid his toys, and he— perhaps understanding that I was tired and grumpy—tried feverishly to entertain me. Listen to all the words I know! Mama, papa, ca (cat), baw (ball), sea (in Italian, *mare*; from Anton's mouth, *mae*), thanks, grama (grandmother), parrot… look how many friends I have: teddy, doll, baby, puppet, puppet, nosy (the rhinoceros), patapa (the platypus), bow-wow bow-wow (the 2 dogs), the mouse with the sombrero, the black crow…. I love that he learned "beach" right away, even though he hasn't yet seen any beach; but I had showed him beaches in pictures and then I must have spoken so enthusiastically that he immediately caught on—and after all, it's an easy word.

In this short account of the night of a mother and child (Anton was about a year old), in this quick sketch of a "competent system," I feel that I can glimpse many typical elements of intersubjectivity: the tensions and joys of mutual recognition, bargaining and sharing, and the co-construction of words (simultaneously given by the parent to the child, and discovered/found by the child). And also an evolutionary emergence: from the primary enjoyment of language (*lalangue*), toward a vocal sound that is no longer just lallation, or babbling, but is not yet language. "It seems fair to add," Zanzotto would say, "a reference to the way in which […] the discovery of the fascination of early landscapes (Ligonàs, Palù, Nino's 'fiefdom'…) very often occurs in a context of primordial, childlike love, with recurring signs of language *petèl*"[15] (the Venetian dialect term for the affectionate baby-talk that a mother uses with a young child, as she approximates the child's own expressive language).

Reading the word *mae/mare* (sea), I feel happy like Winnicott, who says, "the sea is the mother, and on the seashore the child is born."[16] My friend's email—about a woman and child constructing a landscape by teaching each other the words and places they love—brings me back to the idea of motherhood that I discovered, with amazement and admiration, decades ago when I read Jessica Benjamin's early work, where her courageous psychoanalytic discourse braided together feminism and intersectionality and deconstructed gender. It is also to her credit that we have begun to reflect on how the relational discovery of the body, its functions and metaphors, affects the discovery and construction of external reality, and our experience of places and their shapes and the imaginations they produce.

When I think of Meltzer's theories on the "geographic dimension of the mental apparatus,"[17] I wonder about their plausibility for clinical child development—but anyway I am fascinated by their landscape dimension and the image of a continuous exchange between bodies and objects, internal and external:

> In the model of the mind that I am using the geographical dimension can be subdivided, for phenomenological purposes, into six distinct areas: the external world, the womb, the interior of external objects, the interior of internal objects, the internal world, and the delusional system (geographically speaking "nowhere").[18]

"On the seashore of endless worlds, children play" is the line by the poet Tagore that Winnicott sets as an epigram on the seventh chapter of *Playing and Reality*, where he goes on to say that "the sea and the shore represented endless intercourse between man and woman," that "babies come up out of the sea and are spewed out upon the land, like Jonah from the whale," that "the seashore was the mother's body, after the child is born and the mother and the now viable baby are getting to know each other."[19]

Birth and maternal care often evoke the sea and its movement. Sylvia Plath associated the sea with her childhood—something solid and reassuring—but also with her mother—something deceptive and concealing, something that could be seductive and murderous. "The motherly pulse of the sea [...] like a deep woman, it hid a good deal, it had many faces, many delicate, terrible veils. It spoke of miracles and distances; if it could court, it could also kill."[20] And so it was: the killing was a suicide.

Every parent provides their child with an environment. It is the parent's body, their embrace, their smell, their objects and the objects they share. Maybe it's an object with which the child can travel along: inside a baby-carrier sling, in a stroller, on a bicycle, or in a car. Objects that are "thrown into the area of experience with their absolute irreducibility."[21]

The environmental nourishment that comes from this has a definitive effect on our development: it leaves an impression, it triggers potential processes that can only mature if they have what Winnicott calls a *facilitating environment*.

Loewald considers this environment necessary because it contains a "primordial density," a place of experience where all distinctions and boundaries are successively imposed. Mitchell describes it like this:

> Now picture yourself in a large space with several other people and many things all jumbled together. No distinctions exist; everything is yours; there is only yours. Let's call this state of affairs "primary process." Later, you start creating boundaries and borders around some of the other people and things. Some you put in rooms of their own, separate from you. Others you keep in your space. Others are in in-between spaces with two-foot-high room dividers. Let's call this more complexly differentiated state "secondary process." Finally, let us assume that these room dividers are made of some sort of translucent material, so they are both there and not there.[22]

It is here that those objects start to be produced—the objects that Bollas calls evocative and transformative.[23] Objects that shape us while we are also molding them, bending them to our desires. Objects that shape our personality and that we "choose," driven by sensory intuition, formations of compromise between the forms of the psyche and those of things.

> "Did you conceive of this or was it presented to you from without?" asks Winnicott. "The important point is that no decision on this point is expected. The question is not to be formulated."[24]

Character, Bollas says, is an aesthetic move, the Self as a form shaped by a series of chosen objects. If there is a link between how we are and the form we give to our internal world and relationships, we might say that "each of us is a kind of artist with his or her own creative sensibility."[25] The places we seek, as well as those we avoid, express something of our original environmental nurturance. The idiomatic use we make of them will be our poetics.

Why does aesthetic experience imply the feeling of a relationship with the sacred? Why is it that we—like Stendhal in Florence and like

Freud in Athens—when facing an aesthetic object (a poem or a face, a musical phrase or a sunlit sea) feel a sense of surrender and abandonment, a fusion-like impression of loss of boundaries? Because the force of the object captures us in an embrace that represents a primary experience, which precedes language and happens in the body. It's a memory that's *known* but *not thought*, Bollas would say: the memory of a primary process that transforms us. The temporal suspension that characterizes this experience contains the exaltation and the suffering of deep intimacy with the object. What is striking is the sudden eruption of a subversion of sense and senses, like a hierophany (a manifestation of the divine), since one characteristic of the sacred is that "any object becomes *something else*, yet it continues to remain *itself.*"[26] This is not always a positive aesthetic moment: sometimes it is a drugged ecstasy, an addiction that's taken a pathological turn. After all, we learn to know the person who picks us up in their arms (or fails to pick us up) only after they pick us up (or they fail to pick us up).

Winnicott uses the term *transitional* for the material object that's able to satisfy, in the young child, the representation of possession and of the bond with the mother figure. This is a marvelous paradox because the object is precisely transitional: it belongs neither to internal reality nor to the external world. The child has simultaneously found it and created it. A plush toy, the hem of a sheet, a blanket, or a certain smell, sound, or light—these give the comfort of illusion, help with tolerating separateness, invent an intermediate zone, witness the negotiation between internal and external reality, and anticipate the formation of the symbol. In this intermediate area, subjectivity develops in a relationship of mutual dependence between inside and outside. It's a subjectivity that can serve to interpret its own symbols, to mediate between its own thoughts and what it is thinking about, between its own Self and the sensations prompted by experience. One might ask, Ogden suggests, whether it is the emergence of a subjectivity that makes possible the distinction between symbol and symbolized or, rather, whether it is the differentiation between inner (symbol) and outer (symbolized) that allows the emergence of a Self. But this is a misplaced question: "Each makes the other possible, but neither is the cause of the other in a linear sense."[27]

We are still very young when we invent and find transitional objects: those earliest items that are "not-me." But as adults we know that experiences with transitional objects accompany us throughout our lives. At this point, Winnicott writes:

> my subject widens out into that of play, and of artistic creativity and appreciation, and of religious feeling, and of dreaming, and also of fetishism, lying and stealing, the origin and loss of affectionate feeling, drug addiction, the talisman of obsessional rituals, etc.[28]

When I walk on the beach, Winnicott's beach, Tagore's beach, I bend down to pick up stones and shells, feathers and sticks. These objects speak of my connection to the mother, but they also emphasize my connection to the world. They are the transitional objects of the landscape, as for example we see them in Edvard Munch's painting, *Shore with Red House*. Sylvia Plath too wrote about collecting stones and shells, evoking the shimmer of the pieces:

> I pick it up [my vision of the sea], exile that I am, like the purple "lucky stones" I used to collect with a white ring all the way round, or the shell of a blue mussel with its rainbowy angel's fingernail interior; and in one wash of memory the colors deepen and gleam, the early world draws breath. ...Breath, that is the first thing. Something is breathing. My own breath? The breath of my mother? No, something else, something larger, farther, more serious, more weary.[29]

Are they Freudian fetishes? "The fetish" says Freud, "is a substitute for the woman's (the mother's) penis that the little boy once believed in and [...] does not want to give up."[30] But why, Chatwin wonders, the attachment to things? The Freudian idea of fetishism is not persuasive for him. At most, he says, it can be used to interpret the most obsessive forms of collecting. Given that everyone collects items that have symbolism, this collecting cannot be considered a perversion. For a primitive person, every object was a living and mysterious thing that communicated. Trees and stones, he says, spoke to mystics—like Muhammad—and to the depressed—like Gérard de Nérval.[31]

Notes

1 Rilke, Rainer Maria. *Lettere milanesi [Milanese Letters]*, Italian translation, edited by Lavinia Mazzucchetti. Milan: Mondadori, 1956.

2 Benjamin, Walter. *Berliner Chronik [Berlin Chronicle]*, 1932.
3 Freud, Sigmund. "On beginning the treatment," in *Further Recommendations on the Technique of Psychoanalysis*. In *The Complete Psychological Works of Sigmund Freud*. New York, W. W. Norton & Company, 2001, p. 2488.
4 Pontalis, Jean-Bertrand, "Processo o traversata? ["Process or Traversal?]" in *Questo tempo che non passa [This Time That Does Not Pass]*. Italian translation by Giovanni De Renzis. Rome: Borla, 1999.
5 Chatwin, Bruce, and Theroux, Paul, *Patagonia Revisited*. Boston: Houghton Mifflin, 1986.
6 Ferro, Antonino. *La psicoanalisi come letteratura e terapia [Psychoanalysis as Literature and Therapy]*. Milan: Raffaello Cortina, 1999.
7 Ferro, Antonino. *La psicoanalisi come letteratura e terapia [Psychoanalysis as Literature and Therapy]*. Milan: Raffaello Cortina, 1999.
8 Preta, Lorena (ed.), *Cartografie dell'inconscio. Un nuovo atlante per la psicoanalisi [Cartographies of the Unconscious. A New Atlas for Psychoanalysis.]*. Milan-Udine: Mimesis, 2016, p. 15.
9 Szymborska, Wisława. *Map: Collected and Last Poems*. New York: HarperCollins, 2012.
10 Benjamin, Jessica. *The Bonds of Love. Psychoanalysis, Feminism and the Problem of Domination*. New York: Pantheon E-Books, 1988, p. 37.
11 Winnicott, Donald. "The capacity to be alone," in *The Maturational Processes and the Facilitating Environment: Studies in the Theory of Emotional Development*. London: Hogarth Press & the Institute of Psycho-Analysis, 1965, pp. 29–40.
12 Dickinson, Emily, "To make a prairie" in *The Poems of Emily Dickinson: Variorum Edition*, edited by Ralph W. Franklin, Cambridge, MA: The Belknap Press of Harvard University Press, Copyright © 1998 by the President and Fellows of Harvard College. Copyright © 1951, 1955 by the President and Fellows of Harvard College. Copyright © renewed 1979, 1983 by the President and Fellows of Harvard College. Copyright © 1914, 1918, 1919, 1924, 1929, 1930, 1932, 1935, 1937, 1942 by Martha Dickinson Bianchi. Copyright © 1952, 1957, 1958, 1963, 1965 by Mary L. Hampson. Used by permission. All rights reserved.
13 Winnicott, Donald. "Primitive Emotional Development," in *Through Paediatrics to Psycho-Analysis*. London: Tavistock Publications, 1958, p. 152.
14 Benjamin, Jessica. *The Bonds of Love. Psychoanalysis, Feminism and the Problem of Domination*. New York: Pantheon E-Books, 1988.
15 Zanzotto, Andrea. "Il paesaggio come eros della terra [Landscape as the Eros of the Earth]." In *Luoghi e paesaggi [Places and Landscapes]*. Milan: Bompiani, 2013, p. 38.
16 Winnicott, Donald, *Playing and Reality*. London: Tavistock, 1971.
17 Meltzer, Donald. *The Claustrum. An Investigation of Claustrophobic Phenomena*. London: Karnac, 1992.
18 Meltzer, Donald. *The Claustrum. An Investigation of Claustrophobic Phenomena*. London: Karnac, 1992, p. 57.

19 Winnicott, Donald. *Playing and Reality*. London: Tavistock, 1971, p. 129.
20 Plath, Sylvia. *Ocean 1212-W*. London: British Broadcasting Corporation, 1964.
21 Preta, Lorena. *La brutalità delle cose [The Brutality of Things]*. Milan-Udine: Mimesis, 2015, p. 44.
22 Mitchell, Stephen. *Relationality, From Attachment to Intersubjectivity*. New York: The Analytic Press, 2000, pp. 41–42.
23 Bollas, Christopher. *Being a Character: Psychoanalysis and Self-Experience*. New York: Hill and Wang. London: Routledge, 1992.
24 Winnicott, Donald. "Transitional objects and transitional phenomena," in *Through Paediatrics to Psycho-Analysis*. London: Tavistock Publications, 1958, p. 240.
25 Bollas, Christopher. "Interview," in Anthony Molino. *Freely Associated*. London: Free Association Books, 1999, p. 9.
26 Eliade, Mircea. *The Sacred and the Profane. The Nature of Religion*. Translated by Willard R. Trask. New York: A Harvest Book, 1963.
27 Ogden, Thomas. *The Matrix of Mind. Object Relations and the Psychoanalytic Dialogues*. Northvale: Jason Aronson, 1986.
28 Winnicott, Donald. "Transitional objects and transitional phenomena," in *Through Paediatrics to Psycho-Analysis*. London: Tavistock Publications, 1958, p. 233.
29 Plath, Sylvia. *Ocean 1212-W*. London: British Broadcasting Corporation, 1964.
30 Freud, Sigmund. "Fetishism," in *The Complete Psychological Works of Sigmund Freud*. New York, W. W. Norton & Company, 2001, p. 4533.
31 Chatwin, Bruce. "The morality of things," in *Anatomy of Restlessness. Selected Writings 1969–1989*, New York: Viking, 1996, pp. 178–179.

Chapter 3

Being in the world

I used to live in gay sad Paris!
Decades in taxi-honk New York!
Smelly London, watery Venice,
Bright Tanger, and dark Benares!
Now I meditate in the mountains.

Allen Ginsberg, "I used to live in gay sad Paris"[1]

Paris is finished today. I'll live here. My arm no longer flings my soul far away into the distance. I belong.

René Char, "Paris is finished today"[2]

Whoever looks at the landscape shares a promiscuous territory. Dozens of disciplines explore it. Billions of eyes touch it, albeit from different distances. They look at it without being seen. Inhabited or uninhabited, lush or arid, violated or virgin, the landscape is protected (at least here in Italy) by the Constitution, but it remains an indefinable, ambiguous, and boundless object. "It never tires of allowing itself to be defined," but "it is in flight from every possible definition because in itself it encloses all of them."[3] For this reason, too, many authors note the *rhizomatic* characteristic of their landscape studies. This model is different from a tree, which demands a hierarchy, a center and an order of signification—instead, the model is acentric and mobile, like a rhizome, which runs underground and connects things in a subterranean and unpredictable way, bringing into play "very different regimes of signs and even nonsign states."[4] Moreover, the landscape is inhabited by "countless walking brains, by a thousand different but contiguous

DOI: 10.4324/9781003252979-3

mirrors that create it and that, in turn, are continuously created by it."
Landscape is "biologal,"[5] another Zanzottian neologism (a word cob-
bled together from *bios*/life and *logos*/discourse) that indicates an
exchange among landscape, individual and community. Such that the
landscape contributes to the formation of the individual and the community, who in turn enrich the landscape with elements that are not
immediately physical or biological.

To the distanced concept of *landscape* we can add that of *walkscape*,
a passage that is constructed as we walk, as we traverse it with our bodies and our stories. It is a humanized landscape. In order to find ourselves again, we must combine the exploration of the internal world
with that of our landscapes. Walking the landscape is the performative
aspect of a nomadic kind of thinking that makes us appreciate the paths
of actions/words traced by Careri in his work on *walkscapes* (Table 3.1).

The Italian word "paesaggio" (like the French "paysage") is derived
from the Latin *pagus* (village or hamlet): it immediately signals the presence of humans. It is the territory of the village. It becomes the horizon
that one gazes at and it—very often—implies an emotional movement
that's associated with aesthetic requirements.

We can describe the landscape in different ways: if we are looking at
the terrain itself, we might say it is desert or mountainous or glacial or
karst. If we consider the vegetation atop the terrain, we might say it is
forested or steppe-like. If we consider the human aspect, we might speak
of rice paddies or mines or shipping ports.

The geographer Augustin Berque coined the expression *pensée
paysagère* to define not thinking *about* landscape—that is, a concept
that allows it to be identified and represented—but rather a *landscape
type* of thought: a specific sensitivity towards landscape. The idea of
landscape, for Berque, is not universal or ubiquitous: there are in fact
civilizations that are not interested in landscape, in his view, and he
lists criteria that distinguish them from "landscapist" civilizations. For
example, the use of one or more words to say "landscape"; the presence of literature (oral or written) that describes landscapes or exalts
their beauty; an explicit reflection on landscape; the existence of pictorial representations of landscapes; the construction of ornamental gardens; an architecture aimed at the enjoyment of a panorama. In this
sense, a landscapist society that developed well before 15th-century
Europe is the Chinese society of the 4th century, whose language and

Table 3.1 Actions that can be read and acted upon by linking the roles of the three vertical columns. From Careri (2017)

To cross	a territory	to walk
To open	a path	
To recognize	a place	
To discover	propensities	
To attribute	aesthetic values	
To comprehend	symbolic values	
To invent	a geography	to get oriented
To assign	place names	
To descend	a ravine	
To climb	a mountain	
To trace	a form	
To draw	a point	
To tread	a line	to get lost
To inhabit	a circle	
To visit	a stone	
To narrate	a city	
To traverse	a map	
To perceive	sounds	
To guide oneself	through smells	to err
To observe	thorns	
To listen to	ditches	
To celebrate	dangers	
To navigate	a desert	
To sniff	a forest	
To breach	a continent	to submerge
To meet	an archipelago	
To host	an adventure	
To measure	a dump	
To grasp	elsewhere	
To populate	sensations	
To construct	relations	to wander
To find	objects	
To take	phrases	
To not take	bodies	
To tail	people	
To track	animals	
To enter	a hole	to penetrate
To interact with	a grating	
To hurdle	a wall	
To investigate	an enclosure	
To follow	an instinct	
To leave	a station platform	
To not leave	traces	to go forward

pictorial tradition already included specific landscape-words, such as *Shanshui* (meaning, in one word, "the mountains and the waters") or *Fengjing* (meaning "the coming and the light"). These binomials bring into play opposing elements (high and low, movement and vision), creating landscape atmospheres that form suddenly, right before our eyes.[6]

Landscape can be melancholy, enchanting, bleak. Admire the landscape, get lost in the landscape. Landscapes for all, landscapes for the very few. Landscapes devastated by war or by building speculation. The protection of the landscape. Fragile landscapes[7] or lateral landscapes (glimpsed from the window of a car or train). Landscapes in cinema: the indelible *mindscapes* of Visconti's Sicily (*La terra trema*); the foggy Japan of Mizoguchi (*Ugetsu/Tales of Rain and Moon*); the great American West of Dennis Hopper (*Easy Rider*), John Wayne (*Stagecoach*), Michelangelo Antonioni (*Zabriskie Point*), and Alejandro Iñárritu (*The Revenant*); Kubrick's English countryside (*Barry Lyndon*) and Güney's Turkish countryside (*Yol/The Road*); Olmi's Po Valley, reconstructed in Bulgaria (*Il mestiere delle armi/The Profession of Arms*); Herzog's lichens at the end of the world (*Wild Blue Yonder*); Penn's Nordic frost (*Into the Wild*).

Landscapes transformed by art (the practice known as land art): Burri's *Great Cretto of Gibellina* in Sicily, Smithson's *Spiral Jetty* in Utah's Great Salt Lake, Christo's *Floating Piers* in a northern Italian lake—or landscapes reinvented in black and white prints, like the national parks photographed by Ansel Adams in the 1940s.

Introduced at the end of the 16th century, the English word landscape, from the Dutch *landschap*, is a technical term used by painters. Are they, then, the ones who gave landscape its name? The vision of a natural scenario evoked a painted landscape. A country scene, an exotic or picturesque background, depended on their evocative power. So much so that, when people began altering the landscape (with landscape gardening, estate management, and so on) the idea was to achieve a "correspondence" between the "natural" landscape and its pictorial ideal. Again the landscape calls forth the human beings. Participating simultaneously in the external world and the internal world, the painted landscape was a "distant" object that became itself through what the subject—approaching it—projected onto it.

Baudelaire remarked that a grouping of trees, mountains, water, and houses (a landscape) is seen as beautiful not inherently, but because of the idea or feeling that the viewer attaches to it.[8]

One authoritative tradition traces the birth of landscape to the famous letter in which Petrarch recounts his ascent of Mont Ventoux (writing to Father Dionigi di Borgo San Sepolcro). It is a wonderful missive, full of torment and irony, in which the poet contrasts the landscape of the soul to the natural landscape, reproaching himself (with a nod to St. Augustine) for distractedly losing sight of the soul because of the beauty of the nature. Petrarch himself does not seem to believe in this contraposition—and we certainly do not believe in it.

I was rejoicing in whatever success I had enjoyed, I was weeping for my imperfections and I was bewailing the general mutability of human actions. *And I seemed somehow forgetful of the place to which I had come and why*, until, after laying aside my cares as more suitable to another place, *I looked around and saw what I had come to see.* [...] While I was admiring such things, at times thinking about earthly things and at times, following the example of my body, raising my mind to loftier things, it occurred to me to look into the *Book of Confessions* of St. Augustine [...] a handy little work very small but of infinite sweetness. I opened it and started to read at random, for what can emerge from it except pious and devout things? By chance it was the tenth book [...] "And they go to admire the summits of mountains and the vast billows of the sea and the broadest rivers and the expanses of the ocean and the revolutions of the stars and they overlook themselves." I confess that I was astonished, and hearing my eager brother asking for more I asked him not to annoy me and I closed the book enraged with myself because I was even then admiring earthly things after having been long taught by pagan philosophers that I ought to consider nothing wonderful except the human mind compared to whose greatness no thing is great.[9]

The landscape, the anthropologist Meschiari reminds us, "was not born with Petrarch on Mont Ventoux nor in the Renaissance with Flemish painting." Its symbolic form "is an innate mode of thought, an intertwining of cerebral and cognitive structures modeled over hundreds of thousands of years from the sensory experiences of Hominids and *Homo sapiens sapiens* in their respective ecosystems."[10]

If our relationship with the landscape springs from the intersection of perception, cognition, memory, and emotional resonances, the idea of the *mindscape* must contain that of *brainscape*: if we unlink the two, that would impoverish the vision. The visual experience of the land-scape brings us into the territory of a discipline called *neuroaesthetics*, founded by the neurobiologist Semir Zeki. How does our brain "see" objects and their shapes? Is it possible to apply to the vision of land-scape what we have learned from studies on the neural correlates of viewing artistic productions? What does cognitive neuroscience teach us about the way we look at a painting, a sculpture, a film?[11] How much of our perception of landscape is determined by information coming from the outside and how much from our own neural reading? On what do our landscape preferences depend, and how much are they conditioned by the landscape's specific *affordances* (that is, the properties of the object that "grip" our gaze and thereby suggest how to use it)?[12]

Observing the world, writes Vittorio Gallese, is an undertaking more complex than the mere activation of the "visual brain." Visual percep-tion, as we will see in Chapter 5, has a multimodal nature that involves large parts of the brain (sensorimotor, limbic) and therefore must be read in the context of the pragmatic nature of our relations with exter-nal reality.[13]

We know that the neural systems that are activated when we perform an action—or have subjective experience of a feeling or emotion—are also activated when we recognize in others such actions, emotions, and feelings. Even more: the phenomenon of "embodied simulation,"[14] founded on the discovery of *mirror neurons*, also occurs when such actions, emotions, and feelings are shown to the individual, in lab experiments, in the form of static images (e.g., artistic productions). Sensorimotor activation and viscero-motor activation in the brain of the observer are thus—researchers say—responsible for putting the observer "in sync" with what is observed, a tuning-in that helps to explain com-plex phenomena such as empathy, identification, and understanding the intentions of others.[15] So much so that Ramachandran has declared that "mirror neurons will do for psychology what DNA did for biology."[16]

The enthusiasm of Ramachandran, a neuroscientist and scholar of the mechanisms of vision, is related to the application of embodied sim-ulation theory to our aesthetic response to images, including artworks.

Both empathic and aesthetic, embodied simulation is activated in relation to the *content* of an artwork (such as the anguished expressions of the mothers trying to protect their children from stabbing in Guido Reni's *Massacre of the Innocents*, or the finger prodding Jesus' wound in the *Incredulity of St. Thomas* by Caravaggio) and in relation to the traces of the artist's gesture (Van Gogh's brushstrokes, Pollock's drips, Fontana's slashed canvas—and even a vigorous way of shaping clay). Experiments show that even the observation of manipulable objects (for example, a piece of fruit) can stimulate the activation of motor and premotor brain areas that will influence our own interaction with such objects. Static and three-dimensional objects can also be represented in the interaction with an emotionally involved observer. "Even a still-life," say Freedberg and Gallese, "can be 'animated' by the embodied simulation it evokes in the observer's brain." Even an architectural form, they add, can activate this type of response.[17] These are "automatic empathetic responses," to which must be added, of course, any factors that are contextual, experiential, cultural, cognitive, and so on.

Looking at the world is much more than a simple pathway from the stimulus to the retina to the occipital cortex, and every perceptual experience is a bodily experience. But how can we study the vision of natural (not painted) scenarios in light of the hypothesis of embodied simulation? Can we rule out the idea that landscape-viewing activates circuits that predispose us to embodied simulation? An agricultural landscape, for example, carries the trace of human movement: will a plowed field have the same effect on our neurons that a Pollock painting does, or a Rothko? Is this what *land artists* are aiming at, and the *earth workers* who intervene directly on the land, the soil, the territory? How will our brains react when faced with a bucolic or a stormy scene? And how much will depend on the experience and characteristics of the observer—whether s/he is sedentary, a farmer, a mountain climber, a runner, or a scuba diver?

According to recent research,[18] the aesthetic evaluation of artistic products, whether they depict human subjects or natural scenes, implies the spontaneous activation of motor components and therefore of "embodied simulation." Moreover, the detection of an involvement of the posterior insula and central insula leads the researchers to hypothesize that painted natural scenes evoke aesthetic processes that require an additional proprioceptive and sensorimotor component increased by the aspects of "motor accessibility" to the represented scenario which is necessary in formulating an aesthetic judgment of the painting.

A river flows, a wave breaks, a gust of wind kicks up a swirl of sand on a dune, a stork flies overhead, smoke from a chimney blackens the blue sky, a loudspeaker breaks the silence. Landscape can move us and frighten us, placate us or drive us to explore, but it remains—as Searles would say—*a non-human environment*. Contrary to the thinking of the idealistic painter Charles Lacoste, who said that "landscapes have a disposition and a look: nature thinks,"[19] a landscape may indeed mirror our moods and intentions, but it does not itself have moods and intentions. Despite Deleuze's beautiful image of *paysage-visage*, landscape does not present facial expressions. (If anything, the discovery of faces—when we stop to look, traveling in the subway or strolling in the marketplace of a foreign city—can become a landscape experience. We'll come back to this.)

However much or little it stimulates our mirror neurons, landscape is surely not a low-impact event for brain activity; it has always been crucial to our physical adaptation and to our psychic development.

Mountains, oceans, volcanoes, and deserts have long been considered inhospitable and hostile places.[20] Only from the start of the 18th century did these natural locales begin to draw intentional visitors, and begin to be perceived as sublime—endowed with a beauty that was ambiguous, intense, even disturbing. This change explains, in Kantian fashion, the difference between *beauty*, which gives aesthetic pleasure, and the *sublime*, which is perturbing. Kant not only counterposed the aesthetics of the beautiful with the aesthetics of the sublime, but he also distinguished between the *dynamic sublime* and the *mathematical sublime*. In the first case, the limitlessness of nature manifests as extension (for example, in a desert, an ocean, and, typically, a starry sky); in the second case, the limitlessness manifests as power (for example, in a stormy ocean or a hurricane). The sublime landscape can generate a *numinous* experience[21]—to use a term dear to Jungian psychology that indicates the experience of the sacred and the totally other as a *mysterium tremendum et fascinans* (a mystery that is terrifying and fascinating at once).

Remo Bodei wonders if the experience of the sublime is an "aesthetic variant of the apprenticeship to which each person must submit," to deal with the enmity of the natural world and the anguish it sparks in us. Among other functions, it distances us from "quotidian banality," promotes emotional experiences, puts us in touch with deep levels of the psyche, curtails our omnipotent sense of our uniqueness, and tinges "transcendence with immanence." But he cannot help asking whether technological developments, mass tourism, and the domestication or the destruction of the landscape have definitively compromised our possibility of experiencing the sublime.

I'm no explorer, but I'm not a tourist either (although age and caution are making me more of a tourist), and I can see how—in the span of my 50 years as a traveler—the experience of the sublime has been dulled down. Can it be that new comforts, technologies, and supports have shrunk both the *mysterium* and the feeling of *awe* (fear, amazement, intimidation) which, among many other things, is evoked by the pronunciation of the Bionian O?[22] Everything is more domesticated in our eyes, except for the political conflicts and the wars that now grip large portions of the world, making them inhospitable and dangerous (but certainly not in the sublime sense).

Nowadays, the landscape is being transformed by another very palpable threat: rapid climate change. Not the slow, long eras of glaciation or warming that had altered the planet over time, but rather a sinister movement—accelerated, tangible, perceptible from year to year. And for the first time this is happening with the complicity of human intervention. These mutations are born of the exploitation of the landscape, the deforestation of it, and the pollution of it... with poverty and migration as a frequent consequence of this. It is a transformation that distances us from what is domesticated, but without delivering us to the sublime.

The landscape trespasses, it leaps beyond its definition, it cannot be thought of separately from how we perceive it—and from how we imagine it. *Landscape anthropology*, which has developed particularly in Great Britain, looks at the relationship between the subject and the landscape, and tends to focus on the spaces and times of a place in their connection with the physical and cultural activities of the human animal. This co-presence is increasingly defined by anthropologists as *embodied landscape*;[23] the experience of/in the landscape comes to shape every human product, so much so that we could think of landscape as the mental representation of a real place—as Meschiari says, a sort of *forma mentis*.[24] Every sharp distinction between "nature" and "culture" fades away, replaced by a continuous spilling-over. At the same time, the immersion of the body in the landscape implies a split, because it leads us back to the impossible fusion between us and the world, a tension that brings us closer in and further away—an embrace and a distancing—in a form of love that is very similar to Dickinson's:

So We must meet apart—
You there—I—here—
With just the Door ajar
That Oceans are—and Prayer—[25]

and to Rilke's: "when we love we have only this to offer: / to leave each other."[26]

Surprised and suspended in watching, we find ourselves, in Derrida's words:

> when my gaze meets yours, I see both your gaze and your eyes, [...] and your eyes are not only seeing but also visible. And since they are visible (things or objects in the world) as much as seeing (at the origin of the world), I could precisely touch them, with my finger, lips or even eyes, lashes and lids, by approaching you—if I dared come near to you in this way, if I one day dared.[27]

The concept of landscape contains infinite elements, and many of the problems that afflict us today: climate change, environmental decay and pollution, social belonging and social alienation, post-colonialism, migrations, national borders slamming shut, and war. It is heritage and memory of place. The relationship between the human and his or her environment is never "neutral" or unidirectional (whatever the direction). Every time we enter the landscape, we work it, and it works us: individuals, communities, and nations alike. It is a concept in constant tension, and it operates at the root of history and politics, of social relations and cultural representations. It plays on borders and mixes territories. And even if a wall can cut through a landscape, as Trump intended (to halt immigrants at the Mexican border), landscape is stronger than a wall: it will surround the wall. Walls separate, but they are destined to collapse.

Notes

1 "I used to live in gay sad Paris" by Allen Ginsberg. Copyright © 2016 by The Estate of Allen Ginsberg, used by permission of The Wylie Agency LLC.
2 Char, Réne. "Paris is finished today," in *Furor & Mystery and Other Poems*. Translated and edited by Mary Ann Caws and Nancy Kline. Boston: Black Widow Press, 2010.
3 Zanzotto, Andrea. "Verso-dentro il paesaggio [Towards-Into the Landscape]," in *Luoghi e paesaggi [Places and Landscapes]*. Milan: Bompiani, 2013 [1994].
4 Deleuze, Gilles, and Guattari, Félix. *A Thousand Plateaus: Capitalism and Schizophrenia*. Translated by Brian Massumi. Minneapolis: University of Minnesota Press, 1988. © Bloomsbury Academic, an imprint of Bloomsbury Publishing Plc.

5 Zanzotto, Andrea. "IX Ecloghe [Eclogue IX]," in *Poesie e prose scelte [Selected poems and prose]*, Milan: Mondadori, 1999, p. 237. Zanzotto, Andrea. "Il paesaggio come eros della terra [Landscape as Eros of the Earth]," in *Luoghi e paesaggi [Places and Landscapes]*, Milan: Bompiani, 2013, p. 33.

6 Jullien, François. *Living off Landscape*. Translated by Pedro Rodríguez. London: Rowman & Littlefield, 2014.

7 Tarpino, Antonella. *Il paesaggio fragile. L'Italia vista dai margini [Fragile Landscape. Italy Seen from the Margins]*. Turin: Einaudi, 2016.

8 Baudelaire, Charles. *Saggi sull'arte [Essays on Art]*. Italian translation in *Opere*. Milan: Mondadori, 1996, pp. 1009–1353.

9 Petrarch, Francesco. *Letters on Familiar Matters (Rerum familiarium libri)*. Translated by Aldo S. Bernardo. New York: Italica Press, 2005.

10 Meschiari, Matteo. *Terra Sapiens. Antropologie del paesaggio [Terra Sapiens. How Landscape Invented Man]*. Palermo: Sellerio, 2010.

11 Gallese, Vittorio, and Guerra, Michele. *The Empathic Screen. Cinema and Neuroscience*. Oxford: Oxford University Press, 2019 [2015].

12 The term "affordance" comes from Gibson's ecological theory of vision (1979), and indicates those physical properties of an object that suggest with immediacy the appropriate actions for using it. For example, the appearance of a cup with its handle tells the observer how to use it. Even places have their affordances—for example, a beach (you lie down, you walk) or a rock face (you climb it, you lean on it). This is a concept that does not belong entirely to the object or even to the observer: it is created in the relationship between the two. This is a fundamental concept for people who study perception in relation to the exploration of the environment. It carries echoes of Merleau-Ponty's phenomenological considerations (1960) regarding the experience of landscape and how our looking is also a "gripping."

13 Gallese, Vittorio. "The multimodal nature of visual perception: Facts and speculations," *The Kanizsa Lecture*, 38 no. 2/3, pp. 127–140.

14 Freedberg, David, and Gallese, Vittorio. "Motion, emotion and empathy in esthetic experience," in *Trends in Cognitive Sciences* 11, no. 5 (2007), pp. 197–203. Gallese, Vittorio, Eagle, Morris, and Migone, Paolo, "Intentional attunement: Mirror neurons and the neural underpinnings of interpersonal relations," *Journal of the American Psychoanalytic Association* 55 no. 1 (2007), pp. 131–176. Rizzolatti, Giacomo, and Sinigaglia, Corrado, *Mirrors in the Brain: How Our Minds Share Actions and Emotions*. Translated by Frances Anderson. New York: Oxford University Press, 2008.

15 Ammaniti, Massimo, and Gallese, Vittorio. *The Birth of Intersubjectivity: Psychodynamics, Neurobiology, and the Self*. Foreword by Allan N. Schore. New York: W. W Norton & Company, 2013.

16 Ramachandran, Vilayanur S., "Mirror neurons and imitation learning as the driving force behind 'the great leap forward' in human evolution," *Edge*, 2000. www.edge.org/conversation/vilayanur_ramachandran-mirror-neurons-and-imitation-learning-as-the-driving-force.

17 Freedberg, David, and Gallese, Vittorio. "Motion, emotion and empathy in esthetic experience," *Trends in Cognitive Sciences* 11, no. 5 (2007), pp. 197–203.

18 Di Dio, C., Ardizzi, M., Massaro, D., Di Cesare, G., Gilli, G., Marchetti, A., and Gallese, V., "Human, nature, dynamism: The effects of content and movement perception on brain activations during the aesthetic judgment of representational paintings," *Frontiers in Human Neuroscience*, 9 (2016), pp. 1–19.

19 Lacoste, Charles. "La Simplicité en peinture [Simplicity in Painting]," in *La Plume*, 1, 1897.

20 Bodei, Remo. *Paesaggi sublimi. L'uomo di fronte alla natura selvaggia [Sublime Landscapes. Man in the Face of Wild Nature]*. Milan: Bompiani, 2008.

21 Otto, Rudolf. *The Idea of the Holy*. Translated by John W. Harvey. London: Oxford University Press, 1923.

22 About the Bionian O, see Note 6 in chapter 1.

23 Ingold, Tim. *The Perception of the Environment. Essays on Livelihood, Dwelling and Skill*. London: Routledge, 2000. Jones, Ernest. *The Life and Work of Sigmund Freud*. New York: Basic Books, 1953. Lorimer, H., "Cultural geography: The busyness of being 'more-than-representational,'" *Progress in Human Geography* 29, no. 1 (2005), pp. 83–94.

24 Meschiari, Matteo. *Sistemi selvaggi. Antropologia del paesaggio scritto [Wild Systems. Anthropology of the Written Landscape]*. Palermo: Sellerio, 2008. Meschiari, Matteo, *Terra Sapiens. Antropologie del paesaggio [Terra Sapiens. Anthropologies of Landscape]*. Palermo: Sellerio, 2010.

25 "I cannot live with you" in *The Poems of Emily Dickinson*, edited by Thomas H. Johnson, Cambridge, MA: The Belknap Press of Harvard University Press, Copyright © 1951, 1955 by the President and Fellows of Harvard College. Copyright © renewed 1979, 1983 by the President and Fellows of Harvard College. Copyright © 1914, 1918, 1919, 1924, 1929, 1930, 1932, 1935, 1937, 1942, by Martha Dickinson Bianchi. Copyright © 1952, 1957, 1958, 1963, 1965, by Mary L. Hampson. Used by permission. All rights reserved.

26 Rilke, Rainer Maria, "Requiem. Per un'amica [Requiem for a Friend]." Italian translation in *Poesie [Poems] (1908–1926)*, Vol. 2. Turin: Einaudi-Gallimard, 1995.

27 Derrida, Jacques. *On Touching—Jean-Luc Nancy*. Translated by Christine Irizarry. Stanford: Stanford University Press, 2005, p. 3.

Chapter 4

Pockets full of butterflies

Hullo object!

Donald W. Winnicott, Playing and Reality[1]

When she died at 55, she was known to everyone as an expert gardener above all. Emily Dickinson's renown as a poet was to come later. She had written lines including "To be a Flower, is profound Responsibility,"[2] as well as many letters, often with dried flowers tucked inside the paper. Judith Farr[3] tells of Dickinson's relationship with nature, and her love for flowers and wild plants: she was an expert botanist, and she knew their infinite varieties. She had collected them, as an adolescent, in an herbarium—which we could consider to be her first collection of poems. As she was being buried, her younger sister Lavinia put a small bouquet of heliotrope in her hands, and strewed violets and wild orchids around her face. At Emily's behest, the coffin was carried to the cemetery through fields of yellow buttercups. She loved nature—"Nature is Harmony" was the title of one work—but in another poem she remarked, "This is my letter to the World / that never wrote to Me."[4]

"Metaphysical chamber," "melodramatic chamber," "enchanted room," "maternal room,"[5] are the names that the painter Filippo De Pisis assigned to the rooms that served as the backdrop to his imaginative experience. These were places of intimacy, metaphors of the psyche and of memory, which he filled with evocative objects: dried flowers, feathers, shells, mosses, insects, many of them collected during a stroll. In a page of his autobiographical novel (*Il marchesino pittore/The Painter Marquis*), De Pisis refers to a box similar to the herbariums and

DOI: 10.4324/9781003252979-4

the entomological boxes that he loved. Such a box represents an urn in which every biological form is dried, every vivid scrap of memory; he defines it as a box

> of many "objects" [...] of many useless things: feathers, curious bibe-lots, seals, sachets, calendars, semi-precious stones, candles. Small penates that followed him from room to room, from city to city, ever since he—still a pimply and reserved young man—had left his father's home to attend the University of Bologna.[6]

This Ferrarese painter was sketched this way by the writer Raffaele Carrieri:

> His pockets are full of butterflies, of arboreal handkerchiefs, of bee-tles [...]. He speaks of his paintings with great tenderness. He has memories that are very similar to trilling sounds: robins, parrots, tufts of ribbons, flowers, mushrooms, freshly wrapped tissue paper pack-ages, stuffed geese, old-fashioned objects of colored porcelain. Other people have ideas. De Pisis has his nature. A nature that is prehensile, subtle, full of rapid ignitions, voracious, elegant, perceptive, of an absorbing and dilating freshness, rich in vegetable humors and fertile sounds, something gracefully monstrous. He is a painter of sensa-tions. Landscape sensations.[7]

De Pisis's poem "Fiori d'Alpe" (Alpine Flowers) is a true "herbarium of the soul."[8] Amid its dense botanical listings (which include dandelion, arnica, stellaria, epilobium purpureum, inula, pimpinella, myosotis, and so on) certain verses sprout like sorrowful flowers: "In memory, and in the enchantment / of pure light, mountain flowers / tender vegetable essences, you are dear to me, / but a veil of sadness / is not pulled off from you, / as from the maternal caress / forever lost."[9]

Meltzer, as I already mentioned, explains the concept of aesthetic conflict as the "aesthetic impact of the outside of the 'beautiful' mother, available to the senses, and the enigmatic inside which must be construed by creative imagination." He specifically chooses the term "enigmatic," which Laplanche uses to refer to an experience that has strong impact on the child, but which lacks "meaning": eyes and breasts that appear and disappear, a face over which "emotions pass like the shadows of clouds over the landscape."[10] And since the mother is for the child the primordial representation of the beauty of the world (Meltzer says she is both Dante's guide, Beatrice, and Keats' destructive *Belle Dame Sans Merci*), our aesthetic conflict will touch on every aspect of "beauty."

The discovery of beauty gives the child a difficult task: it sparks an "oceanic feeling"[11] of fusion, but exposes the child to separateness, unknowability, and enigma. It is kindled by the sight of the beloved, or a starry sky, or a boundless sea, or an unreachable mountain peak.

> I could caress her, run my hands over her for a long time, but, as if I'd been handling a stone that encloses the saltiness of immemorial oceans or the ray of a star, I felt I was touching only the closed envelope of a being who, through the inside, was accessing the infinite.[12]

Every human, Meltzer says, experiences this conflict for the first time in the relationship with his or her caregiver, and will have to renegotiate it—throughout a lifetime—whenever he or she faces the beauty of the world, or the beauty of a passionate feeling from an intimate bond, or the beauty of an encounter with an artwork, or music, or a landscape. These objects help us to develop our emotional and mental states, to represent in lasting forms the vicissitudes of our inner world.

Bruce Chatwin's *Utz* is a novel about a man who, in order to maintain an illusion, ruined his life by clinging to his collection of figurines. *The Hare with Amber Eyes: A Hidden Inheritance* by Edmund de Waal is the story of a collection of 264 netsuke, small wooden or ivory objects in the form of animals, plants, and gods; of their odyssey from Paris and Vienna to Tokyo; of their tactile transit through the many hands that touched them. "Solid Objects" by Virginia Woolf is a short story about the love for objects that grips a young man in politics. As he strolls on a beach and sinks one hand into the wet sand—"the background of thought and experience which gives an inscrutable depth to the eyes of grown people disappeared, leaving only the clear transparent surface, expressing nothing but wonder, which the eyes of young children display"—his fingers graze "a full drop of solid matter." It is a piece of glass, polished by waves and time. From that moment on, his life will be entirely devoted to the search for admirable objects, pieces of glass or porcelain marked or broken in a curious way; in his passion he would have "ransacked all deposits of earth; raked beneath matted tangles of scrub."[13]

"Thus arise," says Ferenczi, "those intimate connections, which remain throughout life, between the human body and the objective world that we call symbolic."[14]

> I lost teddy bears without a whimper, yet clung tenaciously to three precious possessions: a wooden camel known as Laura, brought by my father from the Cairo bazaar; a West Indian conch shell called Mona, in whose glorious pink mouth I could hear the wish-wash of the ocean; and a book.[15]

A sufficiently good mother (Winnicott would say—and Proust would certainly agree), knows that one of the most difficult moments of a child's day is when he is put to bed.

We rock him, we tell him a story, and our voice, our movements, our presence, help him to get drowsy. The baby falls asleep and we go back to doing our own things. The baby wants to believe that we will stay close to him for a long time—even all night long. In the meantime, he will get accustomed to separation.

Gathering and collecting objects can be a way to re-establish an environment that performs some of the functions that a parent should provide for the child. Objects can be magical and calming; to discover and maintain them can help stabilize identity; they can be tiny anchors of experience that serve to symbolically contain parts of the self.

A patient once told me that he was very disturbed—actually distressed—when a visiting friend inadvertently bumped against a shelf that held a collection of old liquor glasses, and broke two of them.

He often bought these objects in flea markets in various cities and, over time, had become a connoisseur and a minor collector. The associations that followed the story of this episode sparked a sense of broken security, a desperation similar to what he experienced in childhood when his mother, who worked as a tour operator, would leave him and go on one of her trips. Surprised, he saw only now—he told me—that these little glasses, which came from all across Europe and were as fragile and beautiful as his bond with his mother, were compensatory gifts that he gave to himself. Knowing that there were others and would be others—that his collection was potentially infinite and its breadth depended on his choices—was a thought he had never fully realized, but which (he now grasped) had always sustained him. More: he told me that, apart from this main collection, he had collections of objects that he called "childish": minerals, shells, figurines. Gathering, collecting, and preserving items made him feel like the creator of a solid, safe system, but loss or breakage felt like a threat, like the interruption of security and continuity of the environment, like it might make him "go to pieces."[16]

A person who feels (or has felt) that they cannot rely on the stability and familiarity of a human environment that can recognize him, calm him, and value him may resort, episodically or continuously, to a more predictable non-human environment that is available and controllable. Or, more simply, he may want to feel this kind of reassuring feeling at some point in his day, at some point in his life. Emphasizing the importance of collecting as a form of support, Heinz Kohut recounts the case of a young boy who was separated from his parents and placed in an institutional home, where he understood that his parents would not come for him. How did the child struggle not to lose himself completely?

> I discovered this in a particular way: during the period of separation from me, he began to describe the contents of his left trouser pocket. He knew every one of the eight or nine tiny little things that were in that pocket, including a little roll of fuzz that he kept in there. It was just like what he had done with a particular drawer in the children's home, [...] there was one place in this whole world, this one drawer, about which he knew everything.[17]

There is a particular aesthetic intelligence that differentiates us from each other and is articulated by using the objects—material or immaterial, human or non-human—that the environment offers. Each person has their own way of moving, thinking, speaking, and looking, an aesthetic that connotes his or her individuality and character. This elaboration unfolds in the processes of condensations and disseminations that—as in a dream, during a therapy session or a walk—constitute the essence of unconscious creativity. Conscious reflections of these processes are recognizable in the course of free associations or, more simply, in those everyday moments when something strikes you (a memory, a perception) and then you get lost in the thoughts that come to mind in an involuntary and seemingly "meaningless" way. This is a mode of mental functioning that leads us to develop a *separate sense*, so to speak, for relating to reality. In order for this to happen, a certain separateness is needed in turn, a freedom of relationship with the external and autonomous nature of the object that the idiom elaborates in order to elaborate itself.

In the essay "Preoccupation unto Death," Bollas distinguishes among different ways of using objects along a continuum of working though degrees of freedom. Building on his intuition, we could consider those ways to be *obsession*, first of all: that is, a repetitive mental presence that prevents any unconscious use of the object; and then *preoccupation*, understood as anxiously pouncing on something before someone else grabs it; and then *passion*, which—while allowing a certain freedom— can entangle the subject in the beloved object; and simple *concentration*, a generative channeling of interest in an object.[18]

The very practice of mindfulness, that is, the attempt to be alert to one's own thoughts, actions, and motivations, and to suspend judgment, can benefit from a mental immersion in an evoked landscape in order to reinforce the link with the inner landscape. The concept of a "therapeutic landscape" has long existed in literature (Thomas Mann's *Magic Mountain*), and has shaped medical and psychiatric clinical practice (as therapeutic communities are often located purposely in healthy landscapes).

It is fascinating to listen to a patient who compares her attempt to grasp the evolution of her thoughts to the awareness of the changes of light that led Claude Monet to portray the facade of Rouen's Cathedral at different times of day and in different seasons (in his series of 31 paintings done over three years)—capturing variations in light, color, and climate.

Personal objects or collective objects—a family memento, say, or an amulet; a fetish or a totem; an emotional or religious item: I have these in my life, as do we all. We could write pages and pages about them, dwelling on their forms, origins, and consistencies. For example, this is what the biologist Thor Hanson does in telling us stories about feathers, their variety of meanings and their particular transitional function— not only between a human being and an animal, but also between those who walk and those who fly. He wrote a fascinating book that is a "plumarium"[19] about these perfect aeronautical constructions, these prodigies of color and shape. Since the dawn of time, feathers and down have adorned humans and human clothing, tools, and weapons, and have enriched the myths, legends, and symbols of all peoples, from the flight of Icarus to the phoenix.

And then there are the objects that inhabited our youth, that lived in our childhood home with our parents. Suddenly the parents are gone. We are left alone; the family home is an empty house, filled with memories. Some lucky people have sisters or brothers with whom they get along, so they help each other out. You know that house inside out; you were born there. Or maybe you barely know the house, because your mother had recently moved in there. Even in that case, it will still be full of objects that will become part of the grieving process. Objects and people form a kind of single unit that cannot be separated painlessly. Closets, clothes, scents, drawers, tablecloths, combs, photographs, electricity bills, letters, diaries. When a friend of mine is facing this experience, my viaticum is a very small, essential book by a Belgian colleague, Lydia Flem.[20] The title, *The Final Reminder: How I Emptied My Parents' House*, sounds sinister: it sounds like thievery. And that's another association we shouldn't overlook. To empty is to select, to take, to throw away, to give away, to sell. Other people's things that now are our things. Or rather, things that we *seize* in the moment in which they *become* ours. For now, they are suspended in the space between generations. When we are emptying, we are also creating a space— within ourselves; we are re-narrating the past as we sift through it. As we relocate it.

Notes

1 Winnicott, Donald. "Ego integration in child development," in *The Maturational Processes and the Facilitating Environment*. London: Hogarth Press & the Institute of Psycho-Analysis, 1965, p. 120.
2 "Bloom—is Result—to meet a Flower" in *The Poems of Emily Dickinson: Variorum Edition*, edited by Ralph W. Franklin, Cambridge, MA: The Belknap Press of Harvard University Press, Copyright © 1998 by the President and Fellows of Harvard College. Copyright © 1951, 1955 by the President and Fellows of Harvard College. Copyright © renewed 1979, 1983 by the President and Fellows of Harvard College. Copyright © 1914, 1918, 1919, 1924, 1929, 1930, 1932, 1935, 1937, 1942 by Martha Dickinson Bianchi. Copyright © 1952, 1957, 1958, 1963, 1965 by Mary L. Hampson. Used by permission. All rights reserved.
3 Farr, Judith. *The Gardens of Emily Dickinson*. Cambridge: Harvard University Press, 2004.
4 Dickinson, Emily. "Nature is what we see," and "This is my letter to the world," *The Poems of Emily Dickinson: Variorum Edition*, edited by Ralph W. Franklin, Cambridge, MA: The Belknap Press of Harvard University Press, Copyright © 1998 by the President and Fellows of Harvard College. Copyright © 1951, 1955 by the President and Fellows of Harvard College. Copyright © renewed 1979, 1983 by the President and Fellows of Harvard

College. Copyright © 1914, 1918, 1919, 1924, 1929, 1930, 1932, 1935, 1937, 1942 by Martha Dickinson Bianchi. Copyright © 1952, 1957, 1958, 1963, 1965 by Mary L. Hampson. Used by permission. All rights reserved.

5 De Pisis, Filippo. *Il marchesino pittore [The Painter Marquis]*. Milan: Longanesi, 1969.

6 De Pisis, Filippo. *Il marchesino pittore [The Painter Marquis]*. Milan: Longanesi, 1969, p. 9. See also Gerbino, Aldo. "'Fazzoletti arborei,' linfe floreali e piume: Botanica ed entomologia in Filippo De Pisis ['Arboreal handkerchiefs,' Floral Saps and Feathers: Botany and Entomology in Filippo De Pisis]," *Biblioteca di Rivista di Studi Italiani* 33, no. 2 (2015), pp. 90–104.

7 Carrieri, Raffaele. "Filippo de Pisis," *Il Tempo*, Milano, 16–23 January 1941.

8 Gerbino, Aldo. "'Fazzoletti arborei,' linfe floreali e piume: Botanica ed entomologia in Filippo De Pisis ['Arboreal handkerchiefs,' Floral Saps and Feathers: Botany and Entomology in Filippo De Pisis]," in *Biblioteca di Rivista di Studi Italiani* 33, no. 2 (2015), pp. 90–104.

9 De Pisis, Filippo. *Fiori d'Alpe [Flowers of the Alps]* in *Poesie [Poems]* © 2003, Milan: Garzanti S.r.l., Gruppo editoriale Mauri Spagnol.

10 Meltzer, Donald, Williams, Meg Harris. *The Apprehension of Beauty. The Role of Aesthetic Conflict in Development, Art, and Violence*. London: Karnac Books, 1988, p. 22.

11 Freud, Sigmund. *Civilization and Its Discontents*, in *The Standard Edition of the Complete Psychological Works of Sigmund Freud*. London: Hogarth Press and the Institute of Psycho-Analysis, 1953 [1930].

12 Proust, Marcel. *À la recherche du temps perdu: La Prisonnière [In Search of Lost Time: The Prisoner]*, 1923.

13 Woolf, Virginia. "Solid Objects," in *A Haunted House and Other Short Stories*. London: Hogarth Press, 1944.

14 Ferenczi, Sándor. "Stages in the development of the sense of reality." Translated by Ernest Jones. In *An Outline of Psychoanalysis*, edited by J. S. Van Teslaar. New York: Modern Library, 1923, pp. 108–127.

15 Chatwin, Bruce. "I always wanted to go to Patagonia," in *Anatomy of Restlessness. Selected Writings (1969–1989)*. New York: Viking Penguin, 1996.

16 Winnicott, Donald. "Ego integration in child development," in *The Maturational Processes and the Facilitating Environment*. London: Hogarth Press & the Institute of Psycho-Analysis, 1965, p. 57.

17 Kohut, Heinz. *The Chicago Institute Lectures*. Hillsdale, NJ: The Analytic Press, 1996, pp. 87–88.

18 Bollas, Christopher. *Cracking Up. The Work of Unconscious Experience*. New York: Hill and Wang, 1995. See also Lingiardi, Vittorio, and Gazzillo, Francesco. "Il catalogo è questo [Here is the List]." In *Kos, 179–180*, 2000, pp. 18–25.

19 Hanson, Thor. *Feathers. The Evolution of a Natural Miracle*. New York: Basic Books, 2013.

20 Flem, Lydia. *The Final Reminder: How I Emptied My Parents' House*. London: Souvenir Press, 2004.

Chapter 5

Neuroaesthetic landscapes

A trip to Worpswede is a cataract surgery: as if a gray veil (draped between us and other things) suddenly disappeared.

Rainer Maria Rilke, *Worpswede*[1]

It is not my intention to investigate, in ways that would satisfy a neuroscientist, the mechanisms underlying aesthetic appreciation and the emotions that arise. But before I continue, I should share some information from the field of neuroaesthetics in regard to a landscape—that is, wisdom from the field that studies art-making and art-seeing on the basis of anatomy and of the physiology of the mechanisms of vision. Vladimir Nabokov, who was not just the author of *Lolita* but was also a passionate scholar of butterflies, would say that we cannot separate the aesthetic pleasure of looking at a butterfly from the scientific pleasure of knowing what kind of butterfly it is.

I am drawn to empirical research as much as to clinical psychoanalytic work, as long as the former does not narrow down into reductionist readings and as long as the latter does not expand into charismatic or dogmatic attitudes. Scientific knowledge and clinical experience can coexist—indeed, they must coexist. Counterposing general laws against particular cases is not useful, just as it is not useful—in the study of personalities—to set aspects known as "nomothetic" (a taxonomy) against aspects known as "idiographic" (the formulation of a case). Each one needs the other, and it is not true that, as Bion said, the scientific method is adequate only when we deal with "problems associated with the inanimate."[2]

DOI: 10.4324/9781003252979-5

To steal an image from Settis, I would say that the neurologists of vision and the art historians, as well as the cognitive psychologists and the dynamic psychologists, could be seen as teams of excavators—each with their own digging task—who are tunneling into a mountain from opposite sides, but destined to meet "at a certain point."[3] Each one will have their own map: some will have an area of the brain, some will have *Gestalt* psychology and theories of perception, some will be studying context and style, and some will have Bollas' evocative object. Some of the maps indicate paths that are less interesting: I just don't get why people force an artwork and the art-maker onto the shrink's couch to seek their unconscious meanings (while most often stumbling only on their own stuff). Returning to our teams of diggers: the important thing is that the labor is coordinated without preconceptions, and that everyone understands the other people's tasks while being specialized in their own task. *Images of the Mind: Neuroscience, Art, Philosophy*, a volume edited by Lucignani and Pinotti, is a successful dialogue that manages to bridge the gap between neuro-maniacs and neuro-phobics[4] (a gap that is sometimes needed to ignite fresh thinking).

"All visual art must obey the laws of the visual system":[5] this is the phrase that Semir Zeki wrote as he inaugurated *neuroaesthetics* (in an article co-authored with artist Matthew Lamb). With his customary frankness, Zeki declares that "no theory of aesthetics that is not substantially based on the activity of the brain is ever likely to be complete, let alone profound";[6] that the main function of the brain is to acquire new knowledge about the world, and that visual art extends that function; that artists are unwitting neurologists, experts in the mechanisms of vision; that an artwork can be employed, as a kind of luxury testing ground, to investigate the mechanisms of human perception and cognition.

The first rule is that the image does not imprint itself on the retina: it is actually assembled in the visual cortex. So what happens in our brain (because we look with our brain, not with our eyes—as Pliny the Elder had said long ago) when we see a Monet canvas of water lilies, or a storm painted by Turner, or a Rothko color field? What does the history of art teach us about the mechanisms of vision?

And what if, instead of an artist's landscape, we look at a landscape in nature? I have wondered whether, in the inextricable intertwining of perception, cerebral vision, memory, and emotions, neuroscience can also teach us something about our *mindscapes*. After all, understanding the visible with the invisible is a task for neurophysiology, but also for psychoanalysis.

Shortly after the publication of the article by Zeki and Lamb, Lamberto Maffei and Adriana Fiorentini published a book titled *Art and Brain*, thus stretching the interest of the scientific community towards neuroaesthetics and inaugurating a wide-ranging debate.[7] Among the excellent contributors were V. S. Ramachandran (who wrote on the universal laws of figurative art), Jean-Pierre Changeux (on the "activity" of the viewer viewing a painting, his visual path across the canvas, and the attribution of mental states to the characters), and Eric Kandel (tracing his many-decades-long scientific journey through mind, brain, and artistic expression).

And then there is Vittorio Gallese's radically innovative approach, based on the implications of the discovery of mirror neurons and the model of embodied simulation in empathic responses to images in general, and figurative art in particular. With Gallese, the viewer's *whole* body is engaged: its sensorimotor functions, movement, touch, proprioception, hearing, sense of smell. Rather than neuroaesthetics, Gallese prefers an *experimental aesthetics* "where the notion of aesthetics is declined according to its original etymology: *aisthesis*, that is, multimodal perception of the world through the body."[8] He builds on the wisdom of Merleau-Ponty,[9] the idea of a multisensory space all around a person, the body as the subject of perception—a body that is "a bundle of functions, an intertwining of vision and movement."

Others build on the theories of constructivism, *Gestalt* psychology, and Gombrich's project to bring together art and scientific psychology in the study of pictorial representation. Rejecting the idea of the "innocent eye," Gombrich intuited that visual perception—about which so much had been written—is based on classifications and interpretations of information operating at the brain level, thus opening the way to the observer's role, to their contribution to the definition of the artistic product, to the cognitive psychology of art (and to the elements of psychoanalysis introduced above all by Ernst Kris). And, inevitably, to the biology of the aesthetic experience.[10] Here the eye is a "false mirror" as evoked in René Magritte's 1928 painting with that name.

Neuroaesthetics studies the visual brain: how it is stimulated and how it responds to the stimulus through the activation of specialized areas in both the cortex and the limbic area, in processes involving perception and memory. Zeki defines vision as an active process in which the brain must focus only on what it needs to classify objects, without getting distracted by constant changes in context. This requires three separate but interdependent processes: (a) the *selection*, from a wide range of changing information, of what's useful in identifying the constant and essential properties of objects, surfaces, faces, and situations; (b) the *exclusion* of any information that's not relevant for this purpose; and (c) the *comparison* of the selected information to a lifetime of previously stored information, in order to identify and classify the object or scene in question.

Primitive aesthetic is the expression used by Richard Latto, a vision psychologist, to emphasize that the aesthetic pleasantness of a contour or a shape depends on how ancestral and efficient it is, and how easily it can be processed visually.[11] But even the most elementary vision—of a tree, a square shape, a straight line—is a highly specialized cognitive process.

Matisse was right when he affirmed that seeing is a creative endeavor that requires commitment, and that for a painter the simplest medium is the most effective, but also the most difficult. Zeki, in reading artworks by Vermeer, Michelangelo, Malevich, and Picasso neurologically, seems to conclude that visual art is a happy consequence of brain functioning. And he also stresses the temporal dimension: even before we see movement and shape, he says, we see color; and, even before we identify a face, we grasp its expression. The result is a consciousness, or rather "micro-consciousnesses," distributed in space (across the various brain areas that are involved) and time (in the sequence of activity in these areas).[12]

This reference to form, color, and movement leads me onto a little tangent about another landscape that (despite the controversy about its scientific reliability) we can see as a true *mindscape*: Hermann Rorschach's symmetrical inkblot series. Form, color, and movement are in fact the "determinants" originally devised in the coding of the test (the chiaroscuro was added later). The Rorschach test brings together many of the elements discussed here: the characteristics of perception, the presence of "determining" elements, individual peculiarities, and so on. It is, in a certain sense, about encoding in an inkblot our perception of the world: global responses, common details, unusual details, white spaces, elements that are separate or related to one another, form, movement, color, achromatic color, chiaroscuro, reflections, formal quality, symmetry, frequency, human figures (whole / partial / fantasy figures), animal figures (whole / partial / fantasy figures), botanicals, blood, clouds....

And speaking of clouds, Shakespeare, well before Rorschach, had sensed the importance of associations in ambiguous forms:

Hamlet: Do you see yonder cloud that's almost in shape of a camel?
Polonius: By the mass, and 'tis like a camel, indeed.
Hamlet: Methinks it is like a weasel.
Polonius: It is backed like a weasel.
Hamlet: Or like a whale?
Polonius: Very like a whale.

Ramachandran was sitting in an Indian temple, he reports, when he formulated "the ten universal laws of art."[13] This is a series of "aesthetic universals," of operational constants that an artistic object must possess in order to activate the areas of the brain that are responsible for recognizing an object (for example, a female body rather than a male body)—and to do so effectively and across cultures, from Indian Chola dynasty bronzes, say, to Picasso's drawings. If a humanist of vision looks askance at these rules, or an artist who is not inclined to share the general laws looming over their works, Ramachandran emphasizes affably that he does not wish to deny the enormous importance of individual cultures, nor the genius and originality of individual artists, and that even assuming that there are indeed universal laws, which particular law (or combination of laws) is used depends only on the ingenuity and intuition of the artist. There are those who focus on form (such as Moore), those who focus on chromatic spaces (such as Van Gogh or Monet), and so on.

Even animals have preferences in the visual field, according to Desmond Morris and the work by Bernhard Rensch that he cites. Showing a series of cartoons with regular and irregular rhythmic marks to various species of monkeys and birds, Rensch noted that all of the species showed more interest in regular patterns; he interpreted this statistically significant finding to mean that symmetry and repetition were more attractive.

Our visual perceptions are, in short, subject to laws, as shown by an amusing "psychological" experiment conducted by Ramachandran. It is called the "the Bouba/Kiki experiment" and is inspired by a previous study, called Takete and Maluma, carried out by the gestalt psychologist Köhler. Ramachandran shows two images, one pointy and the other rounded, to a group of men and women and asks them to assign to the two images the name "Bouba" or "Kiki." More than 95 percent of people assign the name Kiki to the sharper figure and the name Bouba to the rounded one. This experiment indicates the existence of a link between form, perception, and language. Viewing a sharp figure, moreover, could be associated with specific processes that also involve motor responses, since the "Bouba" sound engages the lips in a softer and more open movement, whereas the "Kiki" sound engages them in a harder, more closed way.

Is a landscape, like a painting or a photograph, also perceived according to invariants that activate neural circuits which then spark responses steeped in subjectivity, dreams, memories, and reflections? Or does it happen only when, for some reason, we are willing to look at it, however lovely or ugly it may be? Viewing a landscape—perhaps even more than a painting—implies the synergy of many "visual apparatuses," including bodily immersion.

In a short essay entitled "Field," John Berger describes the experience of looking at a meadow—the colors, the visual textures, the sounds, the silences—in the two minutes of forced waiting at a railroad crossing. It is a "very precise and immediately recognizable" experience, but it takes place at "a level of perception and feeling which is probably preverbal—hence, very much, the difficulty of writing about it." This experience, says the author, undoubtedly has "a psychological history, beginning in infancy" and is psychoanalytically individual, but it is common in one form or another. "It is seldom referred to only because it is nameless." For me, it is impossible not to add that "field" is a key term in psychoanalysis: it indicates a shared space, a game for playing together (from "dreaming together"), a place to cultivate, but also to continuously transform. It is the space of the analytic relationship. "The field that you are standing before," Berger concludes, "appears to have the same proportions as your own life."[14]

Ocularcentrism in viewing landscape has been criticized, especially by geographers and anthropologists. The landscape experiences of blind people have been studied, for example, starting from what's called a "non-representational" approach, which led to a definition of landscape as the encounter between the forms and materials of which it is composed and the sensitivity with which we perceive them. This raises Merleau-Ponty's famous example, from *The Phenomenology of Perception*: the blind man's cane is an extension of his gaze, an extremity transformed into a sensitive zone. This is a vast theme, ranging from the tiniest of retinal rods to the most branching of neurons, from the landscape reinterpreted by the artist's gaze (Cézanne's poplars or sheaves of wheat; Kiefer's snowy fields) to the most "natural" of Tuscan landscapes (though this too is inevitably "transformed" by the human work of landscaping and by the *mindscaping* that we do).

The discourse is complicated also because the definition of landscape is not univocal, and because of the many ways the landscape can be displayed to us. The argument is well summarized by some questions posed by Settis, not by chance in the introduction to *Art and Brain*:

> What are the perceptual, emotional, mnemonic differences between observing a landscape, or a painting of that same landscape, or a photograph of that same landscape, or a photo of that painting of the landscape? Are they measurable and describable in physiological terms as well as in terms of the history of culture? Do the two approaches lead to comparable and perhaps converging results—or do they have non-overlapping outcomes? Do our minds have objects or mental patterns (innate, or acquired in the earliest months or years of life) that predetermine the forms of perception? [...] Do the most "effective" images become more deeply rooted in the memory? Is this rooting the same for everyone, or is it determined by differences between one culture and another?[15]

Searching for answers, I willingly turn to Gallese's re-reading of the relationship between symbolic expression and aesthetic understanding: he advises us to "look at aesthetics from a perspective centered on the anthropological dimension and its neurobiological substrates, focusing on the relationship between the body-brain and the world." To study the brain-body system it is necessary to understand how our experience of images "is generated by the functional states of our central nervous system, our autonomic nervous system, and by the integration of these two with the cardiorespiratory and muscular system *of an individual with a personal history.*" There's no way not to focus on the "*individual* physiology of the creation and experience of the symbol," nor on, continues Gallese—broadening the discourse to psychoanalysis—"the projective components that characterize our relationship with images, including artistic images."[16]

The possibilities of vision, and the variety of objects that we look at, make any schematic approach unsatisfactory. Let us dwell for example on the different gradations of "vitality" of what we observe. A sparkling sea on a summer day can move us as much as—or more than—a dog watching us while we read, an actress in a film or a play, or the baker who smiles at us when we are buying bread. But the difference between the first example and all the others is the existence of a mental system. Because the dog, the actress, and the baker have something in common with us that no sea—and no landscape—has: a brain and a mind (*pace* the creationists).

And what about works of art? We cannot claim that Antonello da Messina's 15th-century *Portrait of a Man* has a mind (even although the existence of a mind is strongly suggested by the figure staring at us so boldly); and we cannot claim that Caspar David Friedrich's dramatic *Cliffs on the Sea Coast* has a mind (despite the painter's skill in conveying the emotional dimension of "his" stormy landscape).

As the experiments by Gallese's team show, when we observe paintings without any human or animal figures, but with a strong evocation of the artist's creative gesture—for example in the slashed canvases of Fontana or in the decisive brushstrokes of Kline—our motor simulation sets us to reflecting the gestures made by the painter.[17] "What does it mean to look at a painting, a Greek temple, or a film?" wonders Welsh. What does it mean, I might add, to look at an ancient cave painting, a spider by Louise Bourgeois, a work of *land art*, the Guggenheim's white spiral, or a plowed field?

Can we conceive of the astonishment and sense of elevation transmitted to us by the contemplation of a Doric temple or a Gothic cathedral, in purely visual terms? Is it conceivable to divorce the aesthetic experience from our daily motor experience, tactile experience, and viscero-motor experience of reality? Wölfflin claimed no (as did many others, including Merleau-Ponty), and I think that's right. The added value that cognitive neuroscience can bring to the aesthetic debate [...] is manifold. It consists, for example, in *revitalizing the study of artistic and architectural styles, focusing on their biological and embodied roots*. This would make it possible for us to look at a metope or a Corinthian capital with different eyes from those of a modern observer of an artwork, to rediscover in those stylized forms the animal and vegetable roots, merged in the personification of a divinity or of a ritual-sacrificial practice.[18]

The encounter between aesthetics and cognitive neuroscience has changed how we consider the *power of images*, to quote the title of the book in which art historian David Freedberg[19] interrogates the emotional reactions of the spectator before object that requires (or receives) our emotional interest. And so, from the world of macaques (the primates in whom mirror neurons were first identified, in brain area F5, in the early 1990s), the hypothesis of *embodied simulation* (i.e., the activation of various areas of the observer's brain *involved* by simulation, thus in the absence of factual execution, in represented actions or perceived experiences) has risen to the world of humans and has spread into far more refined fields such as aesthetics—with hypotheses and experiments on how our brain responds to artistic images. Seeing a work of visual art or a film is truly a first-person bodily experience that reshapes the primacy of cognition. One crucial element of aesthetic response is indeed the activation of universal embodied mechanisms that include the simulation of bodily actions, emotions, and sensations. "This basic level of reaction to images is essential to understanding the effectiveness both of everyday images and of works of art."[20]

And what about landscape? What must an image be saying in order to activate a mirror experience? Is it essential that there be traces of the human being and his/her mind, face, emotions, or even just a human gesture—like the immediate "tangibility" of a creative gesture? And how much does it depend on our predispositions, intentions, and cognitive organizations? In the "non-human environment," do we merely project—or can we mirror? Is Rilke right to affirm that our relationship with the landscape implies a radical solitude, and only artistic experience can spark a possible encounter?

When looking at a man, we tend to trace many things back to his hands, and trace everything to his face—in which, as on a clock face, we can see the hours that cradle and sustain his soul. *On the contrary, a landscape is just there, without hands and without a face.*[21]

We can get something from the research (already mentioned in Chapter 3) on cortical activations from paintings that have two different types of images (human and natural) in two different situations (static and dynamic). First, it appears there's no difference in cortical activation produced by a human figure instead of a nature scene. Both categories of images, in fact, activate cortical zones that are tasked with the perceptual analysis and classification of the stimulus. Digging into the results of the experiment, we find that paintings depicting human beings, particularly those with dynamic scenes, seem to determine a greater motor resonance (thanks to the actions depicted). Exposure to nature scenes seems to activate an additional sensorimotor component that favors the motor simulation of an imaginary exploratory behavior. In other words, it seems that, in the case of a nature scene, the aesthetic elaboration involves a kind of immersion in the represented scene that's based on the experiences, needs, and emotions of the observer. Viewing an alpine scene will prompt specific activations in a mountain-climber, just as viewing a Hockney swimming pool will prompt specific activations in a swimmer... but, in conclusion, I think it is that our neurons are quite interested in the landscape.

According to Michael Gazzaniga, a psychologist and neuroscientist, we have *innate* preferences for landscape.[22] Children, on average, prefer a savanna landscape, while adults split equally: half of them choose the savanna and half choose what is most familiar to them. Among the favorites overall are landscapes with trees, particularly trees with spreading canopies (the African savanna type)—and this also seems to apply to people who grew up in areas with mostly round or pointed trees. (This research was conducted by showing photographs of a tropical rainforest, a deciduous forest from a temperate climate, a forest of conifers, a savanna, and a desert.) In general, people seem to prefer landscapes that include water and/or vegetation. But when this option is removed, other preferences become apparent. Hospitalized patients with views of trees through their windows seem to improve faster and require less pain medication than patients who see just walls outside their windows.

Gordon Orians, Emeritus Professor of Biology at the University of Washington, proposes an explanation known as the "savanna hypothesis": the aesthetic responses in favor of trees with extended forms come from an innate knowledge of the kinds of trees associated with productive human contexts in our ancestral habitats.[23] By analyzing our aesthetic preferences for landscapes, and for natural contexts in general, from an evolutionary perspective, Orians concludes that our experience of the natural world is not accidental. Even our aesthetic relationship with the natural environment, he says, is immersed in the history of our evolution. Many of our aesthetic preferences, from how we build a garden to the shapes we love having around us, are the persistent result of natural selection. Darwin taught us that many of our reactions (fear of snakes, revulsion at cockroaches, disgust at a rotten-egg smell) are rooted in the neurological lives of our ancestors, who lived in natural environments where it was essential to recognize danger in order to protect themselves. Fear, revulsion, and disgust—as well as positive emotions, probably, corroborated by a sense of gratification and thus a desire to repeat them—mark our evolutionary history. But Proust and Freud have shown us how many non-phylogenetic variables complicate and personalize the picture.

Speaking of frameworks, it's worth mentioning the curious experiment that Orians reports, done by the artistic duo Vitaly Komar and Alexander Melamid, Russian dissidents who are now American citizens. The pair asked a marketing agency to research the visual preferences of a large sample of American adults. The pollsters asked about a thousand people various things including: What is your favorite color, the one that you would like to have as most prominent in a painting to hang in your home? Would you prefer to have a painting with wild animals in it, or domesticated pets? A portrait, or a nature scene? Geometric patterns or random patterns? Angles or rounded surfaces?—and so on. After analyzing the responses and identifying the most common ones, Komar and Melamid incorporated the favorite images in a single landscape painting that they titled *America's Most Wanted*. It is a savanna-like landscape, with a tranquil lake, hills in the background, a predominance of blues, two deer, shrubs, a tree that is easy to climb, three young people, and an older man: George Washington!

The two artists conducted the same experiment in nine other countries (Russia, Ukraine, France, Finland, Denmark, Iceland, Turkey, Kenya, and China) and obtained surprisingly similar landscapes. As for the other questions, the majority of responses indicated preferences for paintings of pleasant outdoor scenes painted with harmonious colors. Other preferences for the "most wanted" included animals (both wild and domestic) and human figures, especially women and children, in natural poses.

As in America, in these other countries the presence of "familiar" historical figures took on a positive meaning. The two artists could only comment that at the beginning of their work, they believed that freedom meant breaking free from clichés and seeking a personal style. "Looking for freedom, we found slavery."[24]

In short, most people dream of a quiet life, away from danger and protected by positive figures. And there's nothing new about that: it may not seem very adventurous (who knows how Ulysses or Gandhi would have responded to the poll?); it seems modest and not at all courageous. But, at least from an evolutionary viewpoint, these are the ancestral roots of adaptation. Few explorers and many families? Jane Austen, who was no evolutionary biologist, but was a courageous woman, seemed to understand their point of view, as is clear in this passage from *Sense and Sensibility*:

> The first part of their journey was performed in too melancholy a disposition to be otherwise than tedious and unpleasant. But as they drew towards the end of it, their interest in the appearance of a country which they were to inhabit overcame their dejection, and a view of Barton Valley, as they entered it, gave them cheerfulness. It was a pleasant fertile spot, well wooded, and rich in pasture. After winding along it for more than a mile, they reached their own house. A small green court was the whole of its demesne in front.
>
> [...] The situation of the house was good. High hills rose immediately behind, and at no great distance on each side; some of which were open downs, the others cultivated and woody. The village of Barton was chiefly on one of these hills, and formed a pleasant view from the cottage windows.[25]

Then again, in all mythological and religious accounts of the afterlife, Heaven is a place of meadows, trees, and fountains, and Hell is a place of swamps, craters, fires, and mists. Nothing like a savanna, Orians would say. Hieronymus Bosch's triptych, the *Garden of Earthly Delights*, illustrates this: even in its enigmatic symbolic complexity, the earthly garden is green and fruitful and fertile, and the place of damnation is gloomy and smoky. (And it is striking that some of these imaginary constructions in the first two panels of the triptych resemble cards VIII, IX, and X of the Rorschach test.)

Much research in the field of evolution indicates that humans have a predisposition for an "ideal landscape." According to Stephen Kaplan, most people, regardless of cultural background, prefer images of natural environments over man-made environments; moreover, all research in environmental psychology supports a widespread preference for savanna-like landscapes. These are, as we have already summarized, environments that contain hills, semi-open spaces, rivers and lakes, trees with wide branches and—in the distance—an area suitable for exploration. We keep coming back to the same conclusion: there is a parallel between people's preferences and the environmental circumstances in which humans first settled.

Attachment to places is an interdisciplinary research area that has boomed since the 1990s with an examination of not only the components of place-attachment (cultural, social, and psychological components, etc.), but also the variety of environments involved (from small objects, to immediate contexts such as the home, to extended spaces such as communities, cities, and large landscapes). Cognitive psychology, too, explores the mechanisms by which we assign meaning to a landscape, and we grab hold of it, producing scientific works with curious titles such as "Differences in rural landscape perceptions and preferences between farmers and naturalists," or "Children's landscape preferences: From rejection to attraction," or "Fractal dimension of landscape silhouette outlines as a predictor of landscape preference." Of the endless and somewhat repetitive literature, I will report on a few investigations—noting first that much of the research has developed around the question of how our perception is swayed: are we moved more by information from external stimuli, or by personal conceptualizations and personal interpretations? Although my chief interest is the role of landscape in determining meanings, memories, and affections, I tend to think that we won't get very far if we distinguish between the perceptual properties of the environment and their individual psychological significance. As I read the research that I have tried to summarize in this chapter—work that uses photos to study the existence of environments and landscapes that are "averagely preferred"—I wondered: but will photographs be enough? Being immersed in a space, in its light, its odors, in the landscape's own movements... how would that modify the outcome of these experiments? Many of these studies, although fascinating, do make me want to stress again—on the topic of landscape preference and place identity—the complexity and specificity of the elements involved: those that are evolutionary, biological, psychological, and (it goes without saying) ethnic and cultural.

That there is a shared way of looking at the landscape, based on generalizable preferences, is nevertheless a stimulating concept. Some research, for example, has established that we possess hierarchically structured knowledge systems in the form of environmental patterns stored in our memory. This hierarchy functions at different levels of abstraction, from the pattern of *all natural landscapes* to *all forested landscapes* and all the way down to (for example) *the undergrowth of a beech forest*. According to this hypothesis, our preference for a landscape results from the encounter between a given sensory input and our prototypical *landscape archives*. In search of a cognitive ecology of landscape, and starting from the idea of a "personal geography," Farina and Belgrano[26] introduce the concept of the *eco-field*, meaning a spatial configuration that carries meaning and is recognized for a specific function (for example, where to look for food, or—for a bird—where to roost).

Rachel and Stephen Kaplan, who study landscape preferences, point to four "general" elements that can predict preferences: coherence (the degree of concordance and harmony between elements), legibility (the ease with which a landscape can be categorized), complexity (the variety of elements that make up the landscape scene), and mystery (the hidden variables that don't spark fear but do fuel exploration). Here too, water and greenery are seen as important attractive elements. Starting from what's called Attention Restoration Theory, the Kaplans also try to identify some characteristics that are the basis of preferences dictated by the need for rest and regeneration: the *distance*, both physical and conceptual, from the everyday environment; simple *fascination* (for example, drifting clouds, leaves in the breeze, burbling water); the *extent* of the space; and the *compatibility* with one's interests or inclinations. Their theory is based on the belief that the urban environment forces an excess of attention—continuous and stressful—on a task, while the natural environment allows attention to be spread out over the space in a relaxed and soothing way.[27] The Kaplans' research on restorative environments has influenced the work of urban planners and architects, promoting the greening of urban spaces ranging from the Promenade

Plantée (la Coulée Verte) in Paris to the High Line in New York City, the Goods Line in Sydney, and the planned Green River project in Milan.

"Identity and place" is a theme that has engaged anthropologists and geographers for a few decades now,[28] and they have accustomed us to thinking and living the landscape as a dynamic and embodied experience, scaling back the attempt to understand our responses to landscapes by means of experiments that show two-dimensional images of standard landscapes: generic seas, mountains, savannas, forests. Paralleling this (indeed, synergistically), environmental psychologists now immerse themselves in the study of our relationship with the environment—understood as space, nature, climate, social and political structure—trying to understand our cognitive maps, the relationship between public and private spaces, deprivation and attachment to places.[29]

For John Tooby and Leda Cosmides, every stage of development and adaptation has an aesthetic component. The behavior motivated by aesthetic aspects, they argue, can seem non-utilitarian only if we analyze it in relation to adaptive changes that affect the external world and not the internal world of the brain, its pleasure, and its gratifications. Their evolutionary theory of beauty indicates that what we find beautiful probably contains clues to something to which (in the environment in which we evolved) it might have been satisfying to direct our "sustained sensory attention"—even in the absence of utilitarian motives. Fortunately, Tooby and Cosmides—without limiting what we can appreciate aesthetically—assert that some categories follow fairly codified principles: among them, sexual attractiveness and landscape. Moreover, they believe that there are exemplary patterns of pleasantness and relaxed pleasure against which we "measure" our level of comfort in our context. If the agreement is high, we are able to relax, but as soon as the environmental stimuli deviate from expectations, our attention is reactivated.[30]

"What is it about natural landscapes that attract the brain? Can you say fractals?"[31] Gazzaniga asks. "Many natural objects have what is known as fractal geometry, consisting of patterns that recur at increasing magnification. Mountains, clouds, coastlines, rivers with all their tributaries, and branching trees all have fractal geometry, as do our circulatory system and our lungs." If we do an experiment where we show fractal and non-fractal patterns, 95 percent of people will prefer the fractal ones—obviously without knowing that they are fractal. To be precise, they prefer scenes with a low level of complexity, scenes where D (density of fractals) equals 1.3—and they display a lower stress response during the experiment.

Gazzaniga therefore hypothesizes that hospital patients recover better and faster if they have a "room with a view." If they see a garden through their window, in fact, they can count on a natural pattern of fractals equal to 1.3 D.

Physicist Richard Taylor has tried to figure out what kind of "agreement" there is between fractals and vision. Why does our visual system prefer fractals of certain specific dimensions? How does it "recognize" them amidst all the chaos of nature? According to Taylor: (a) when we examine a scene, the first things we process are the contours of objects, and (b) contours play a fundamental role in the perception of fractals. Therefore, the meeting point between the eye and fractals could be the silhouette[32]—a hypothesis supported by the discovery that people tend to prefer horizon lines with fractal values of 1.3!

In short, all this research demonstrates the existence of objects and landscapes whose structure influences our tastes and our reactions. So it is plausible that we prefer fractals in the way we look at objects. Moreover, as Kandel explains—as he traces the history of the study of vision mechanics—many experiments show our particular preference for certain shapes, and therefore the particular ability of a painting to strike us. So much so that one could write a history of art-viewing based on the formal characteristics of the work. After all, as Freud said, even before he came along, poets understood the existence of the unconscious; and Peter Brook argued that those who make theater "already knew" that mirror neurons exist; likewise, Zeki declared that painters are the greatest neurologists of the visual system.

But to leap from here to saying that our whole relationship with the landscape can be reduced to visual neurobiology (understood as a preference for figures that require less discriminative effort, such as symmetrical shapes)—that's a big leap. Such an assertion would be a *pensée de survol* ("high-altitude thinking"), to cite the term used by Merleau-Ponty when he warned against the kind of modern scientific thinking that transforms things into "objects in general," instead of embodying them in their enigmatic concreteness. When we look at the landscape, we don't see just a rigid and repetitive series of stimuli that produce stereotyped responses in us, in a narrow repertoire. What we see is actually an infinite array of possibilities that can combine into an infinite set of *mindscapes*. Neuroscientists themselves remind us that we do have genes that encode certain adaptations, but the potential of those genes can develop only when unpredictable external conditions are met. That "our evolved inheritance is very rich compared to a blank slate, but very impoverished compared to a fully realized person."[33]

Although immediate aesthetic attractions exist, and are predictable and biologically determined, the question "can science provide us with universal and genetically determined guidelines to explain our aesthetic aesthetics?" gets an answer of "No." Even though our preferences may be dictated by the pull toward symmetry and toward easily processed information, still our aesthetic inclination is much more complex, intertwined, biographical. All we have to do is hear a first-person account of the story of a landscape, and we can grasp the leap from a fractal to an evocative object: here are the words of a great artist, Claudio Parmiggiani—

Everything was rooted in the earth and in myth; memory continually turned toward death, toward pity, toward war.[...] A cart pulled by oxen, carrying the bodies of two men who were shot on the shore of a pond covered with waterlilies: that is one of my earliest memories. I learned the color of blood before I learned the colors of oil paints. I was born in Luzzara, in a house on Via Lino Soragna. Much of my childhood was spent in the remoteness of the countryside, in a red house, a very isolated house. [...] From that place I received the best teaching for painting. At night, along the starry canals, the slow water—cradling the melancholic moon—fed the absolute fire. [...] I have memories from those places of slow, black boats and men like shadows who transported sand and fog. Those shadows are my symbol; the floating spirits that in my mind have taken on the immutable appearance of the soul. Shadows so distant that they transmute into everything and nothing. I have done nothing, over the years, but try to grant a sense and an image to that nothingness. Everything that subsequently appeared in my work comes from those early, decisive, indelible images that are, really, the only ones that count—and that are born from emotion, the true source of art.[34]

Notes

1 Rilke, Rainer Maria. *Worpswede* [*Worpswede*]. Italian translation. Milan: Claudio Gallone, 1998.
2 Bion, Wilfred. *Learning from Experience*. London: Karnac Books, 1984, p. 14.

3 Settis, Salvatore. "Introduzione [Introduction]," in *Arte e cervello [Art and the Brain]*, edited by Lamberto Maffei and Adriana Fiorentini. Bologna: Zanichelli, 2008.

4 Lucignani, Giovanni, and Pinotti, Andrea. *Immagini della mente. Neuroscienze, arte, filosofia [Images of the Mind. Neuroscience, Art, Philosophy]*. Milan: Raffaello Cortina, 2007.

5 Zeki, Semir, and Lamb, Matthew. "The neurology of kinetic art," *Brain* 117 (1994), pp. 607–636.

6 Zeki, Semir. *Inner Vision: An Exploration of Art and the Brain*. Oxford: Oxford University Press, 2003, p. 1.

7 For a critical review, see Cappelletto, Chiara, *Neuroestetica. L'arte del cervello*. Rome-Bari: Laterza, 2009.

8 Gallese, Vittorio. "Arte, corpo, cervello: per un'estetica sperimentale [Art, Body, Brain: For an Experimental Aesthetics]," *Micromega* 2 (2014), pp. 49–67.

9 Merleau-Ponty, Maurice. *Phenomenology of Perception*. Translated by Donald A. Landes. London and New York: Routledge, 2012.

10 Gombrich, Ernst. *Art and Illusion: A Study in the Psychology of Pictorial Representation*. London: Phaidon Press, 1960.

11 Latto, Richard. "The brain of the beholder," in *The Artful Eye*, edited by Richard Gregory, John Harris, Priscilla Heard, and David Rose. Oxford: Oxford University Press, 1995, pp. 66–95.

12 Zeki, Semir. *A Vision of the Brain*. Cambridge: Blackwell Scientific Publications, 1993.

13 Ramachandran, Vilayanur. *The Emerging Mind: The Reith Lectures*. London: Profile Books, 2003. The laws are: 1. Peak shift, 2. Grouping, 3. Contrast, 4. Isolation, 5. Perception problem solving, 6. Symmetry, 7. Abhorrence of coincidence/generic viewpoint, 8. Repetition, rhythm and orderliness, 9. Balance, 10. Metaphor.

14 Berger, John. *About Looking*. New York: Pantheon Books, 1980.

15 Settis, Salvatore. "Introduzione [Introduction]," in *Arte e cervello [Art and Brain]*, edited by Lamberto Maffei and Adriana Fiorentini. Bologna: Zanichelli, 2008.

16 Gallese, Vittorio. "Arte, corpo, cervello: per un'estetica sperimentale [Art, Body, Brain: For an Experimental Aesthetics]," *Micromega* 2 (2014), p. 65.

17 Umiltà, Berchio, Sestito et al. "Abstract art and cortical motor activation: An EEG study," *Frontiers in Human Neuroscience* 6 (2012). www.frontiersin.org/journals/human-neuroscience/articles/10.3389/fnhum.2012.00311; Sbriscia-Fioretti, Berchio, Freedberg et al., "ERP modulation during observation of abstract paintings by Franz Kline," *Plos One* 8, no. 10 (2013), e75241.

18 Gallese, Vittorio. "Arte, corpo, cervello: per un'estetica sperimentale [Art, Body, Brain: For an Experimental Aesthetics]," *Micromega* 2 (2014), pp. 49–67.

19 Freedberg, David. *The Power of Images. Studies in the History and Theory of Responses*. Chicago: The University of Chicago Press, 1989.

20 Freedberg, David, and Gallese, Vittorio, "Motion, emotion and empathy in esthetic experience," *Trends in Cognitive Sciences* 11, no. 5 (2007), pp. 197–203.

21 Rilke, Rainer Maria. *Worpswede* [*Worpswede*]. Italian translation. Milan: Claudio Gallone, 1998. The italics are mine.

22 Gazzaniga, Michael S. *Human. The Science Behind What Makes Us Unique.* New York: Harper & Collins, 2008.

23 Orians, Gordon H. *Snakes, Sunrises, and Shakespeare. How Evolution Shapes Our Loves and Fears.* Chicago: University of Chicago Press, 2014.

24 Wypijewski, JoAnn. *Painting by Numbers. Komar and Melamid's Scientific Guide to Art.* New York: Farrar, Straus & Giroux, 1997.

25 Austen, Jane. *Sense and Sensibility*, 1811.

26 Farina, Almo, and Belgrano, Andrea. "The eco-field hypothesis: Toward a cognitive landscape," *Landscape Ecology* 21, no. 1 (2006), pp. 5–17.

27 Kaplan, Stephen. "The restorative benefits of nature: Towards an integrative framework," *Journal of Environmental Psychology* 15 (1995), pp. 169–182.

28 Owain, Jones, and Garde-Hansen, Joanne. *Geography and Memory. Explorations in Identity, Place and Becoming.* Basingstoke: Palgrave Macmillan, 2012; Taylor, Stephanie. *Narrative of Identity and Place.* New York: Routledge, 2010.

29 Baroni, Maria Rosa. *Psicologia ambientale [Environmental Psychology]*. Bologna: Il Mulino, 2008.

30 Tooby, John, and Cosmides, Leda. "Does beauty build adapted minds? Toward an evolutionary theory of aesthetics, fiction and the arts," *Substance* 30 (2001), pp. 6–27.

31 According to a general (non-mathematical) definition, a fractal is a geometric figure or natural object with the following characteristics: (a) each of its parts has the same shape or structure as the whole, but on a different scale, and slightly deformed; (b) its shape is highly irregular or fragmented, and remains that way, whatever the scale at which it is examined; (c) it contains "distinct elements" whose relative dimensions are varied and diverse. Gazzaniga, Michael S. *Human. The Science Behind What Makes Us Unique.* New York: Harper & Collins, 2008, p. 229.

32 Hagerhall, C., Purcell, T., and Taylor, R. P. "Fractal dimension of landscape silhouette as a predictor for landscape preference," *Journal of Environmental Psychology*, 24 (2004), pp. 247–255.

33 Tooby, John, and Cosmides, Leda. "Does beauty build adapted minds? Toward an evolutionary theory of aesthetics, fiction and the arts," *Substance*, 30 (2001), pp. 6–27.

34 Parmiggiani, Claudio. *Incipit [Incipit]*. Turin: Umberto Allemandi & Co., 2008; see also Recalcati, Massimo. *Il mistero delle cose. Nove ritratti d'artista [The Mystery of Things. Nine Artists' Portraits]*. Milan: Feltrinelli, 2016.

Chapter 6

Face and landscape
("that's where I would like to live")

So, is your mother a landscape or a face?

Gilles Deleuze, Félix Guattari, *A Thousand Plateaus*[1]

[Melville] even pined for Home and Mother, the two things he had run away from as fast as ships would carry him. HOME and MOTHER. The two things that were his damnation.

D. H. Lawrence, *American Classics*[2]

Roland Barthes organized old photographs of his mother soon after she died. "Straining toward the essence of her identity, I was struggling among images partially true, and therefore totally false." He happened to pick up a photo of his mother as a child which, because of its setting, he calls "Winter Garden Photograph": in that moment he *found* her again: it's her. He recognized "the impossible science of the unique being." Raised as a Protestant, without Catholicism's adoration of the maternal image—and yet inevitably influenced by Catholic art—Barthes saw that photo and he surrendered "to the Image, to the Image-Repertoire."

But we never got to see the photo. For us, it would not make sense: "It exists only for me."[3]

A few lines later we read something beautiful that reveals the "landscape" element of a beloved face: his mother's picture, Barthes wrote, is "literally an emanation of the referent"; it "will touch me like the delayed rays of a star." His mother's face touches him with luminous properties: "[It] is for me the treasury of rays which emanated from my mother as a child, from her hair, her skin, her dress, her gaze, on that day."[4]

DOI: 10.4324/9781003252979-6

Your soul is a chosen landscape.[5] What if a landscape was indeed like a face? What if our way of looking at landscape creates a fantastical kinship with the face of our childhood caretaker? What if Zambrano was right when she declared that "sleep and wakefulness are not two parts of life," because life has no parts, but has "only *places* and *faces*"?[6] What if Deleuze and Guattari grasped an actual possibility when they stated that the face has "a correlate of great importance: the landscape"? (Surely they were not referring to the caricatural tradition—of Johann Christian Vollerdt in the 1750s, and other painters—that translates landscapes anthropomorphically into faces.)

> Face and landscape manuals formed a pedagogy, [...] and were an inspiration to the arts as much as the arts were an inspiration to them. Architecture positions its ensembles—houses, towns or cities, monuments or factories—to function like faces in the landscape they transform. Painting takes up the same movement but also reverses it, positioning a landscape as a face, treating one like the other: [...] The close-up in film treats the face primarily as a landscape; that is the definition of film, black hole and white wall, screen and camera. [...] So, is your mother a landscape or a face? A face or a factory? (Godard.) All faces envelop an unknown, unexplored landscape; all landscapes are populated by a loved or dreamed-of face, develop a face to come or already past. What face has not called upon the landscapes it amalgamated, sea and hill; what landscape has not evoked the face that would have completed it, providing an unexpected complement for its lines and traits?[7]

Any research aimed at deepening the intersubjective relationship between child and caregiver[8] highlights the centrality of faces as the main way of recognizing the other and our (mirrored) selves. This centrality is also emphasized by all studies on the psychology of visual perception and the biology of emotional responses of people observing artworks containing human figures. Among the stimuli that we perceive, faces are the most informative: a single glance is enough to capture the age, gender, ethnicity, state of mind, and directed-attention of a person nearby. The system that governs face perception occupies a very important space in our brain, more than other recognition systems.

The ability to recognize faces depends on specific face-selective brain regions. Experiments conducted using functional magnetic resonance imaging (fMRI) have revealed specific areas of the cortex responsible for the visual perception of faces (the Fusiform Face Area, or FFA). A lesion in this area is believed to be implicated in prosopagnosia (face-blindness). It's a disorder that Oliver Sacks himself lived with, and he wrote compellingly about it; with his reserved humor, he told how his face-blindness had caused many diplomatic stumbles—for example, when he failed to recognize his analyst on the street (and the analyst took it as a hostile gesture that Sacks didn't greet him).[9]

Doris Tsao, Margaret Livingstone, and Winrich Freiwald have done complicated research studies on monkeys and demonstrated the existence of "face patches" that have specific functions in facial recognition. Face patches belong to an articulated system of connections with other brain areas that, in humans, depend significantly on the amygdala.[10]

In general, writes Kandel, the visual system creates cerebral representations (in the form of neural codes) "that require far, far more information than the modest amount the brain receives from the eyes."[11] The fact that the brain "adds" a whole range of information is the basis of the assertion by Chris Frith—a cognitive psychologist—that "our perception of the world is a fantasy that coincides with reality."[12] This illusion of coincidence should not, however, reduce images to a purely cerebral fact. Rather, it should prompt the question about where Me ends and where the rest of the world begins. "We are involved—that is to say, tangled up—with the places we find ourselves," notes Alva Noë, a philosopher and theorist of perception. "We are not like the berry that can be easily plucked, but rather like the plant itself, rooted in the earth and enmeshed in the brambles."[13]

Among the associations Jung reported in the course of his experiments on affective tone complexes, the word "paint" elicits "landscapes" as the first reaction.

The patient clarifies: "One paints landscapes, portraits, faces—also the cheeks when one has wrinkles."[14] This phrase reminds me of an exhibition that I saw a few years ago: *Lineaments: Face and Landscape*. In the catalog, the artist, Tullio Pericoli, spoke of his pleasure in painting a landscape as if he were portraying a face. Faces and landscapes become maps that are transformed with time. To know, as Zanzotto would say, "one's own obscure marriage / with the sky and the woods."[15]

"Copying from nature is meaningless to me," wrote Egon Schiele, "because I paint better pictures from memory, as a vision of the landscape—now I mainly observe the physical movement of mountains, water, trees and flowers. Everywhere one is reminded of similar movements made by human bodies, similar stirring of pleasure and pain in plants."[16]

When we look at a landscape, we establish a dialogue with the evocative objects that populate it. We recognize them and relocate them, connecting perception, memory, and affections. Rilke, though, thought that the distance between face and landscape was unbridgeable, because nature was absolutely extraneous and indifferent: the landscape "is there, with no hands, and with no face, or—rather—it is nothing but a face, and it is a face so grand, with such immense features, that it frightens and discourages man." But he was forced to rethink his position when he pointed to art as the possible location for an encounter between man and landscape, the answer to a reciprocal pull. Which makes the artist paint a human portrait "as if it were a landscape" and paint a "landscape without figures" in which everything seems to speak of "the one who has seen it."[17]

I wrote about the face of my woman friend—her face speaks to me of a landscape, and a landscape speaks to me of her face:

Delicately Lappish,
then harshly Aegean,
it was not mimicry
but the face of the landscape
that made you my goddess.[18]

Barthes's words return to speak to us of the bond between desire and landscape. Once again, he is looking at an old photograph—this time it is a picture not of his mother, but of a house, an old photo of a house taken by Charles Clifford in 1854 in the Alhambra in Granada.

What does the French semiologist see? "An old house, a shadowy porch, tiles, a crumbling Arab decoration, a man sitting against the wall, a deserted street, a Mediterranean tree...." The photograph moves him and prompts him to feel that it is simply *there:* that's where I would like to live. The roots of this deep desire are unknown to him: "warmth of the climate? Mediterranean myth? Apollinism? Defection? Withdrawal? Anonymity? Nobility? Whatever the case (with regard to myself, my motives, my fantasy), I want to live there, *en finesse.*"[19]

The consonance is a pleasant attunement, a musical harmony and a coincidence of consonants. What attracts Barthes in a place is habitability, not visitability. In a quick note written elsewhere, he confesses to being unable "to interest myself in the beauty of a place if there are no people in it (I don't like empty museums)." In a sort of reciprocity, he goes on to say that "to discover the interest of a face, of a figure, of a garment, to savor the encounter," he requires that "the site of this discovery have its interest and its savor as well."[20] In short, just as he doesn't like empty museums, he doesn't like faces out of context.

His "longing to inhabit" is not traceable to an oneiric dimension ("I do not dream of some extravagant site") or an empirical dimension ("I do not intend to buy a house according to the views of a real-estate agency"). It is a "fantasmatic" desire that he describes as "a kind of second sight which seems to bear me forward to a utopian time, or to carry me back to somewhere in myself."[21]

Looking at these landscapes of predilection, it is as if I were certain of having been there or of going there. Now Freud says of the maternal body that "there is no other place of which one can say with so much certainty that one has already been there." Such then would be the essence of the landscape (chosen by desire): *heimlich*, awakening in me the Mother (and never the disturbing Mother).[22]

Freud's passage that inspires Barthes refers to dreams and landscapes, making the comparison even more attractive:

> In some dreams of landscapes or other localities emphasis is laid in the dream itself on a convinced feeling of having been there once before. (Occurrences of "déjà vu" in dreams have a special meaning.) These places are invariably the genitals of the dreamer's mother; there is indeed no other place about which one can assert with such conviction that one has been there once before.[23]

When speaking of his *clairvoyance*, Barthes evokes this "double movement which Baudelaire celebrated in *Invitation au voyage* and *La Vie antérieure*": "landscapes of predilection" where we are sure that we have been—or must go. Time and memory, the aesthetic pleasure of some stimuli and the unpleasantness of others, combine to establish our environmental satisfactions, our sense of emotional attunement or disattunement with the environment. And there is the *consonance*: "I want to live there." And where Barthes limits himself to a timid "warmth of the climate,"[24] the more euphoric Pasolini proclaims: "My heart beats with joy, with impatience, with orgasm. Alone, with my Fiat 1100 and the whole South in front of me."[25] One hundred and fifty years earlier, Stendhal felt such a high "peak of emotion" in Florence's Basilica of Santa Croce that he swooned with dizziness and a pounding heart—so much that people still today speak of "Stendhal's Syndrome" (an illness that's more literary than medical).

While we explore the environment, our attention lingers on certain objects, creating a territory of "affective markings" and "aesthetic indexations"[26] that remain wrapped in a temporality that includes the past (in the form of memory) and the future (in the form of expectation). All these aesthetic constellations—that "Mediterranean tree," that "crumbling Arab decoration," and also "the whole South," perhaps concentrated in an agave or in a clay wall—these constellations trace (and inhabit) the map of our evocative objects. Different disciplines contribute to describing the formation of our subjectivity within primary relationships characterized by salient moments of shared attention with aesthetic connotations.[27] The child discovers and explores the world, and therefore also himself, from within an affective relationship that will leave evidence, will leave emotional marks on objects: the face of the other, parts of his own body, objects that are close and tangible, objects that are distant and elusive. The child first wants to sample an object by putting it in his mouth; later, he learns to merely point to the object; and then the object can simultaneously belong to both the child and the landscape. "In the smile and its opposite (the grimace of disgust) is thus anticipated—with corporeal expressiveness—the basic condition of every future aesthetic judgment."[28]

Aesthetic propensity thus sits between needs and predetermined functions and the advent of the environment, which begins to take shape as a landscape dotted with attractors, where one can exercise preferences and evaluations with respect to how things perceptually appear. This is a movement that seeks to reconcile the known and the unknown, the near and the far: the security of the familiar and the excitement of the explorable. The landscape will call us to express that aesthetic attitude that has been built up through mirroring, adjusting, and dialoguing with the face of the person who cared for us.

When we are in a theater or an airport, in a bar or in a foreign country, other people's faces can also become landscape. They too will have aesthetic markers—affective or erotic markers—that speak differently to each of us (or that remain silent): prominent ears, monolid eyelids, short stature, flushed cheeks, thin lips, large hands, small breasts, gappy teeth, complexions pale as dawn or dark as night. Barthes calls it

> the huge dictionary of faces and figures in which each body (each word) means only itself and yet refers to a class; hence one has both the pleasure of an encounter [...] and the illumination of a type (the feline, the peasant, the apple, the savage, the Lapp, the intellectual, the sleepyhead, the moon-face, the smiler, the dreamer), source of an intellectual jubilation, since the unmasterable is mastered.[29]

In these fetishisms of the *visual* landscape (of vision and of the visage), there will be different degrees of obsession, different degrees of object-processing.[30] One can use eye color as the basis for an anthropological theory, as Lawrence does:

> There is something curious about real blue-eyed people. They are never quite human, in the good classic sense, human as brown-eyed people are human: the human of the living humus. About a real blue-eyed person there is usually something abstract, elemental. Brown-eyed people are, as it were, like the earth, which is tissue of bygone life, organic, compound. In brown eyes there is sun and earth and shadow and soaked water. But in blue eyes there is principally the abstract, uncreate element, water, ice, air, space, but not humanity.[31]

Or one might focus on the impact of faces—as did Pasolini, who gazed at figures who might have been painted by Masaccio, in the archaic outskirts of Rome: figures "with white cheeks [...] and dark circles under the eyes from the times of primroses, of the first barbarian invasions." Or again in Kenya, where Pasolini discovered "other cheekbones [...] other foreheads [...] other noses," where "Beauty is Beauty, and does not lie" and is reborn "among curly, flat-nosed souls."[32]

Psychoanalysis "has scarcely anything to say" about beauty, said Freud. But one thing is sure: the link between beauty and sexual attraction. And since the genitals, "the sight of which is always exciting, are nevertheless hardly ever judged to be beautiful," beauty ends up being attributed to "certain secondary sexual characters."[33] "The merits of a sexual object are described as 'attractions.'"[34]

Let's look again at Barthes' dislike of the empty museum. He jotted down this note, and I read it nearly 30 years ago (I had, in turn, jotted it in my own notebook—but in my memory I transformed it into a comment about the sadness of an unviewed gallery of portraits); finding his remark again, now, prompted me to re-read the entire collection of those small Barthesian texts. They turned out to be a treasure trove. The first part of the book is titled "The Light of the Sud-Ouest," and it begins like this:

> Today, July 17, the weather is splendid. Sitting on the garden bench and squinting so as to obliterate all perspective, the way children do, I see a daisy in the flowerbed, flattened against the meadow on the other side of the road.

Once again, we see a spatiotemporal subversion and the choice of an element, light, that allows us to travel from the smallest detail (the daisy) to the most distant and intangible object (the light):

> Then begins the great light of the Sud-Ouest, noble, and subtle at the same time; never gray, never low [...], it is light-as-space, defined less by the colors it imparts to things [...] than by the eminently habitable quality it communicates to the earth. [...] You must see this light (I would almost say: hear it, so musical is its quality).

If anyone were to object—why is it that "all you talk about are things like the weather, vaguely esthetic or in any case purely subjective impressions [?]. But the people, their relations, industries, commerce, problems...?"—the answer would be expected: because *"to read" a land means chiefly to perceive it according to the body and the memory, according to the body's memory.* For this reason, our childhood is the royal road to knowing a land. "Ultimately," Barthes concludes, "there is no Country but childhood's."[35]

Francesco is a teacher in his fifties, intelligent, witty and melancholic. He often speaks to me of a place from his childhood and adolescence that is real but also a mythical location: the Meadows of Castel Maggiore (I'm using a pseudonym here). He went there for the first time with his parents, in what he views as the sunny era of his childhood. His physical and emotional vitality stayed there, in the memory of this place that had a Whitman-esque splendor. As he grew, he made a psychic refuge of that place, his *Heimat* far from home, an Eden outside of "the real world" which he had learned to inhabit and own, but which he had stripped of every desire. In the Meadows, though, nature was "gilded" in a way that reverberated in his identity, not only as security, but actually as physical and psychic wholeness. When he began analysis with me, his connection with life lay in the lost heroism of this ancient *mindscape*, outside of which the world paled. We talked at length about the Meadows, and of course about everything else: his childhood, his mother's paralyzing intrusiveness, his father's indifferent shyness, the shame of his body that felt alien to him, and his sexuality that did not nourish him. After a few months of analysis, he decided to return to his trips to his personal Eden, almost as if he wanted to make contact with the boy "who was no longer and would no longer be." By losing himself and rediscovering himself in those Meadows, he was able—in the course of his therapy—to re-establish contact with his child's/teenager's body that his mother had taken possession of.

The places of our childhood can represent a lost Eden, as well as a landscape that bears the signs of the conflicts and fears that life continues to present. My colleague tells me about a patient who returned to her small hometown in Northern Italy, after many years away. Moving through the locations she had left 20 years earlier, places which lived on, in her imagination and her memory, as both fairytale-like (because she had been a child) and oppressive (because of her parents), brought her to a new experience in her analysis. "Finding myself there," she said, "among the woods and mountains where I used to play as a child, I had a sharp, clear perception. Those places belonged to me, but I no longer belonged to them." Commenting on this clinical exchange, my colleague tells me that, for the patient, this experience was a metaphor that helped her to grasp a new way of being in the world—and it was also the first step toward the conclusion of her long journey with my colleague.

No one is immune to the power of places, immune to their violence, sweetness, indifference. We live in tension between origin and destination, transitory or definitive, desired and sought or imposed by political, economic, and family circumstances. Between the *motherland* (homeland) and the urge to separate—as in our youth when we negotiate our needs for autonomy and dependence. Our greater physical freedom (when we can move away on our own two feet) makes us aware of our physical separateness—and we are simultaneously curious and frightened.

We are migrants; always have been. The migrations are fueled by "material needs and immaterial aspirations."[36] We can explore the world, but we don't want to give up the safety of eye contact. Inhabited by the illusory memory of a wonderful, lost world, we traverse hostile and distracted landscapes. We walk forward, but we turn to look back. How have we been looked at, in that moment?—With anguish, concern, defiance, anger, or envy? Or maybe we have simply not been looked at? How blind, or devastated, was our mother's home? Throughout our lives, this experience will condition our relationship with places and their objects. This relationship will also be a consequence of how we handled the "aesthetic conflict," according to Meltzer's adage that "in the beginning was the aesthetic object, and the aesthetic object was the breast, and the breast was the world."[37] Sensitive to beauty and to its enigmatic fragility, the infant thus begins "to write its poetry and paint its pictures of a world scintillating with meaning."[38]

Notes

1 Deleuze, Gilles, and Guattari, Félix. *A Thousand Plateaus: Capitalism and Schizophrenia*. Translated by Brian Massumi. Minneapolis: University of Minnesota Press, 1988, p. 172. © Bloomsbury Academic, an imprint of Bloomsbury Publishing Plc.

2 Lawrence, D. H. *Studies in Classic American Literature*. New York: Thomas Seltzer, 1923, p. 126. Reproduced with permission of the licensor through PLSclear.

3 Barthes, Roland. *Camera Lucida. Reflections on Photography*. Translated by Richard Howard. New York: Hill and Wang, 1980, pp. 66, 70, 71, 75, 73.

4 Barthes, Roland. *Camera Lucida. Reflections on Photography*. Translated by Richard Howard. New York: Hill and Wang, 1980, p. 82.

5 Verlaine, Paul. *Fêtes galantes [Gallant Festivals]*. Paris: L. Vanier, 1896.

6 Zambrano, María. *Chiari del bosco [Forest Glades]*. Italian translation. Milan: Feltrinelli, 1991. The italics are mine.

7 Deleuze, Gilles, and Guattari, Félix. *A Thousand Plateaus: Capitalism and Schizophrenia*. Translated by Brian Massumi. Minneapolis: University of Minnesota Press, 1988, p. 172. © Bloomsbury Academic, an imprint of Bloomsbury Publishing Plc.

8 Approaches to this research range from the innate proto-conversational readiness of the infant highlighted by Colwyn Trevarthen to Ed Tronick's still face paradigm, and from Daniel Stern's intonation profiles to the microanalyses of face-to-face communication conducted by Beatrice Beebe.

9 Sacks, Oliver. *The Mind's Eye*. New York: Alfred A. Knopf, 2010.

10 Livingstone, M. S. "Mechanisms of face perception," *Annual Review of Neuroscience* 31, 411–437. Tsao, D. Y. "A dedicated system for processing faces," *Science*, 314 (2006), pp. 72–73. Tsao, D. Y., and Freiwald, W. A. "What's so special about the average face?" *Trends in Cognitive Sciences* 10, no. 9 (2006), pp. 391–393. Freiwald, W. A., Tsao, D. Y., and Livingstone, M. S. "A face feature space in the macaque temporal lobe," *Nature Neuroscience* 12, no. 9 (2009), pp. 1187–1196.

11 Kandel, Eric. *The Age of Insight. The Quest to Understand the Unconscious in Art, Mind, and Brain*. New York: Random House, 2012.

12 Frith, Christopher. *Making up the Mind. How the Brain Creates Our Mental World*. Madden: Blackwell Publishing, 2007.

13 Noë, Alva. *Out of Our Heads: Why You Are Not Your Brain, and Other Lessons from the Biology of Consciousness*. New York: Hill and Wang, 2009, p. 69.

14 Jung, Carl Gustav. *Psychology of Dementia Praecox*. Princeton: Princeton Legacy Library, 1974, p. 46.

15 Zanzotto, Andrea. "Nella valle, Dietro il paesaggio [In the Valley, Behind the Landscape]," *Le poesie e prose scelte [Selected Poems and Prose]*. Milan: Mondadori, 1999, p. 107.

16 From a 1913 Egon Schiele letter to Franz Hauer: Steiner, Reinhard, *Egon Schiele, 1890–1918. The Midnight Soul of the Artist*. Köln: Taschen, 2004.

17 Rilke, Rainer Maria. *Worpswede [Worpswede]*. Italian translation. Milan: Claudio Gallone, 1998.

18 Lingiardi, Vittorio. *Alterazioni del ritmo [Alterations in the Rhythm]*. Rome: Nottetempo, 2015.

19 Barthes, Roland. *Camera Lucida. Reflections on Photography*. Translated by Richard Howard. New York: Hill and Wang, 1980, p. 38.

20 Barthes, Roland. *Incidents*. Berkeley: University of California Press, 1987, p. 45.

21 Barthes, Roland. *Camera Lucida. Reflections on Photography*. Translated by Richard Howard. New York: Hill and Wang, 1980, p. 40.

22 Barthes, Roland. *Camera Lucida. Reflections on Photography*. Translated by Richard Howard. New York: Hill and Wang, 1980, p. 40.

23 Freud, Sigmund. "The Interpretation of Dreams," in *The Complete Psychological Works of Sigmund Freud*, Vol. 1–24. Translated by Ernest Jones. New York, W. W. Norton & Company, 2001, p. 856.

24 Barthes, Roland. *Camera Lucida. Reflections on Photography*. Translated by Richard Howard. New York: Hill and Wang, 1980, p. 40.

25 Pasolini, Pier Paolo. *La lunga strada di sabbia [The Long Road of Sand]*, © 2017, Ugo Guanda Editore S.r.l., Milan.

26 Desideri, Fabrizio. *La percezione riflessa. Estetica e filosofia della mente [Aesthetics as Perception Reflected. Aesthetics and the Philosophy of Mind]*. Milan: Raffaello Cortina, 2011.

27 Meanwhile, other salient experiences in one's relationship with one's care-givers help organize development: these are *ongoing regulations* (i.e., the patterns—positive or negative, but always predictable—in which the dyad regulates communications); *disruption and repair* (where expectations are dashed, but there is the possibility that regulation can resume); and *height-ened affective moments* (which can foster or generate state changes). Beebe, Beatrice, and Lachmann, Frank M., "Representation and internalization in infancy: Three principles of salience," *Psychoanalytic Psychology* 11, no. 2 (1994), pp. 127–165.

28 Desideri, Fabrizio. *La percezione riflessa. Estetica e filosofia della mente [Reflected Perception. Aesthetics and Philosophy of Mind]*. Milan: Raffaello Cortina, 2011.

29 Barthes, Roland. *Empire of Signs*. Translated by Richard Howard. New York: Hill and Wang, 1970, p. 96.

30 See, in Chapter 4, the various levels of fruition of objects suggested by Bollas.

31 Lawrence, D. H. *Studies in Classic American Literature*. New York: Thomas Seltzer, 1923, p. 126. Reproduced with permission of the licensor through PLSclear.

32 Pasolini, Pier Paolo. *La Guinea [Guinea]*, in *Poesia in Forma di Rosa [Poems in the Form of a Rose]*, © Garzanti Editore s.p.a., 1964, 1976; © 1999, 2001, Garzanti S.r.l., Milan.

33 Freud, Sigmund. *The Standard Edition of the Complete Psychological Works*, Vol. 1–24. London, The Hogarth Press and the Institute of Psychoanalysis, 1953–1974, p. 4481.

34 Freud, Sigmund. *Three Essays on the Theory of Sexuality*, in *The Complete Psychological Works of Sigmund Freud* Vol. 1–24. Translated by Ernest Jones. New York, W. W. Norton & Company, 2001, p. 1475.

35 Barthes, Roland. *Incidents*. Berkeley: University of California Press, 1987, pp. 4–5, 6, 9.

36 Calzolaio, V., and Pievani, T. *Libertà di migrare. Perché ci spostiamo da sem-pre ed è bene così [Freedom to Migrate. Why We're Always Moving and It's OK to Do So]*. Turin: Einaudi, 2016.

37 Meltzer, Donald. *Studies in Extended Metapsychology: Clinical Applications of Bion's Ideas*. Perthshire: Clunie Press, 1986, pp. 244–245.

38 Meltzer, Donald, and Harris Williams, Meg. *The Apprehension of Beauty: The Role of Aesthetic Conflict in Development, Art and Violence*. New York: Karnac Books, 1988, p. 14.

Chapter 7

Amor loci

Who will not know it, this surviving land,
how will they understand us? Say who we have been?
But it is we who must understand him,
so that he may be born, though lost to these clear days,
to this stupendous stasis of winter,
in the sweet and stormy South, in the North that is covered in
    shadow…

Pier Paolo Pasolini, For Bertolucci¹

In *Aida*, in the third-act duet, Radamès and Aida weigh the future of
their love. Aida, the enslaved Ethiopian woman, rejects Radamès, the
Egyptian warrior who loves her but who is betrothed to Amneris, the
Pharaoh's daughter. "I could not love you if you lied to me," sings Aida.
Radamès reassures her: once the war is won, he will tell the Pharaoh of
his true feelings and will ask Aida to marry him. Aida knows that this
plan won't work ("You don't fear Amneris's vindictive furor?") and
invokes the only viable solution: escape. The idea becomes a landscape:
"Let us flee the harsh passions of these barren plains," she suggests.
"A new homeland will welcome our love. There, among virgin forests,
perfumed with flowers, in blissful ecstasy shall we forget the world."

This marvelous aria sets the desolation of a loveless captivity, in an
inhospitable and desolate land, against the promise of happiness in a
new homeland—fragrant and hospitable—that's ready to welcome their
love. On one hand is the negative *mindscape* in Egypt (barren plains,
slavery, death) and on the other hand is the positive one in Ethiopia
(fragrant flowers, freedom, love). Radamès hesitates, and Aida rejects

DOI: 10.4324/9781003252979-7

him again. Then they cleave to one another again, and pain and hope seem likewise to cleave together as one, in the landscape.

Continuing the duet with the same notes, however, Radamès goes on speaking of his Egypt ("the *endless deserts* shall be our bridal chamber, the stars will shine on us with unusual brilliance") while Aida looks to her Ethiopia ("*fresh valleys* and *green meadows* shall be our bridal chamber, the stars will shine on us with unusual brilliance"). The landscape challenge launched by Aida (harsh passions in barren plains versus blissful ecstasy in perfumed forests) could be quashed by Radamès, who might envision in Aida's beloved locales only skies full of rheumatic dampness, rotting flowers, and buzzing insects. His locale is the desert: the yellow sand, the soft dunes, lovemaking in a tent set in a cool oasis laden with dates.

While I listen to *Aida*, I follow the thread of my landscape thoughts, sparked by Ghislanzoni's libretto. My thoughts drift off from the Pharaonic story and into ideas about the pull of places, their psychic meaning. Into the fact that, yes, we often use the landscape "only" to reflect our emotional states—the ideal place to situate, more or less poetically, one of our states of mind. (We could call this a *landscape-mirror*.) But a *mindscape* is much more: it is already alive in us. It is an imagination, Bachelard would say, that "enhances the values of reality."[2] It is like falling in love; the face in which we seek out / create that place that already dwells within us, because, as Siegmund sings in *Die Walküre*, "You are the picture that I was hiding in myself." It is not just our gaze alighting on the landscape; it is also the landscape entering into our gaze and transforming it. (We could call this a *landscape-psyche*). It is when the fullness of a place touches—even painfully—the deepest sense of our personality.

I think of landscapes in the history of art, first as a *background* for human events (shards of impracticable and abstract places in medieval paintings; glittering peaks in Venetian paintings; enigmatic rural scenes—green with water and blue with fog—behind the figures in Leonardo da Vinci's works) and then as the *protagonist* of the canvas, at one with the artist: the magical sense of waiting in Giorgione's *Tempest* or the luminous peace of Monet's water lilies (which were donated to the city of Paris to help its citizens rediscover the solace of a garden after the pain of World War I). My thoughts struggle against two things: both the easy but untenable opposition between landscape-nature and landscape-culture, and the equally unsustainable opposition between "dehumanized" landscape (total otherness) and "humanized" landscape (the sublime extension of our states of mind).

Verdi's music knocks me out of my schematizations... and I am grateful for it. Radamès reveals—such a betrayal!—that his army was going to swoop down on the enemy through the gorge of Nàpata. Again, my thoughts wander off to a sentence from a book I have just read, *The Naked Tourist*. While flying over a forest, the protagonist, who is also the author, Lawrence Osborne, says that his eyes fill with a green that gradually becomes a psychological greenness. I think of the love of wilderness that governed the lives of men like Wilfred Thesiger and women like Gertrude Bell.

I think of Conrad's South Seas. I think of Darwin's Patagonia: these treeless expanses, considered lifeless by most people, gripped the great naturalist more than did the pampas, which are greener, more fertile, and perhaps more useful to humanity.

Last, I think about myself, and about how for many years, mountain excursions seemed foreign to me. Amid cows and conifers, I felt like Osborne above Wanggemalo: "Those huts, that path, the swarming forest—it was not a part of my psyche."[3] But I was always ready for any southern plains. Like Caetano Veloso, *vuelvo al Sur como un destino del corazón*: I return to the South as a destiny of my heart.

Rome and all Italy, Greece, and Egypt are all psychic territories that are fundamental for understanding Freud.[4] In a letter to his wife from Lavarone in Northern Italy, he asked himself:

> So why are we leaving this ideally calm, lovely place with its wealth of mushrooms? Simply because there is only a week left, if that, and our heart, as we have observed, points to the south, toward the figs, the chestnuts, the laurels, the cypresses, the homes adorned with balconies, the sellers of antiquities, and all the rest.[5]

The letter is dated September 1900; Freud had already been in Italy, but not yet in Rome. For several years the Italian capital had hovered as a forbidden dream for him: it was a lure that was ambivalent and—as he wrote to Fliess—"deeply neurotic."[6] In the *Interpretation* he recounts "a series of dreams which are based upon a longing to visit Rome" and some incidents marking the impossibility of reaching the city (incidents that he reads through a lens of Oedipal conflict and of cultural and religious affiliation). Rome was a symptom. To get there, he had to become an archaeologist of his self and, through dream analysis, to bring out the Rome that lay within himself. "A great love for and an invincible phobia about Rome," concluded Musatti.[7]

Freud ended up visiting the city seven times from 1901 through 1923, tirelessly.

> Arriving in Rome after two o'clock, I changed at three o'clock, after my bath, and I became a Roman. [...] It is incredible that we have never come here before. Noon in front of the Pantheon: that's what I have feared for years. It's almost deliciously hot, and this is related to the fact that a stupendous light is diffused everywhere, even in the Sistine Chapel. Otherwise one lives divinely, if one is not forced to exhaust oneself in being thrifty. Water, coffee, food, bread: excellent [...]. Today I stuck my hand in the *Bocca della Verità*, swearing that I would come back here. [...] Roman women are strangely beautiful, even when they are ugly. [...] Never have I lived so long without working, following only my whims and desires. [...] Too bad you can't always live here. [...] My plan for old age is certain: not a cottage, but Rome.[8]

Freud's Rome is a landscape of evolutionary archaeology, and of psychic and religious intertwining, and of femininity (at the Vatican Museum, Freud—having read Jensen's story—bought a reproduction of the bas-relief of Gradiva), and of masculinity (he went again and again to the Church of San Pietro in Vincoli to see Michelangelo's Moses: he tried to "stand up" to the statue's "frowning and contemptuous look" but he sometimes just "crept cautiously away in the penumbra"). Rome was to open his way *toward the south*: to Naples, Pompeii, Ravello, Paestum, Positano, Palermo, and Agrigento. Turning to the South, he wrote Élisabeth Roudinesco, his gaze merges "with the magnetized compass-needle that directs him—a traveler lost among his ghosts—to head toward a land similar to the immense expanse of the unconscious."[9]

In 1904 it was time for Athens. His biographer Ernest Jones recounted that Freud dressed in his best shirt to ascend the Acropolis, and that the visit surpassed any other experience he had ever had or imagined; indeed, two decades later he said again that the amber columns of the Acropolis were the most beautiful thing he had ever seen.[10]

On the Acropolis he was seized by a crisis of derealization, "a sense of some feeling of the unbelievable and the unreal in the situation at the moment," and he asked his brother Alexander, his travel companion, if they really *were* on the Acropolis. Freud described the episode many years later—with an Oedipal interpretation once again—as feeling crushed by a sense of guilt for having reached such a long-desired goal. As if he had realized an impermissible desire. He whispered in his brother's ear Napoleon's words on the day of his coronation: "What would *Monsieur notre Père* have said to this, if he could have been here today?" To reach such a distant place, whose beauty his parent might not even have understood, showed him the "limitations and poverty" of his family of origin. When his consciousness faltered, he realized that his "longing to travel was no doubt also the expression of a wish to escape from that pressure, [...] to run away from home." The conflicting knot was made up of his wish to outdo his father: "It seems as though the essence of success was to have got further than one's father, and as though to excel one's father was still something forbidden." So, he concluded (in this letter marking Romain Rolland's 70th birthday), "what interfered with our enjoyment of the journey to Athens was a feeling of filial piety."[11]

Do we need more personal reports to understand the psychic power of the landscape—what it can gather from our stories and what we can absorb from its own stories? Like a dream that strikes us, or a face that strikes us, landscapes too supply our psychic functioning with images. A psychoanalyst must get to know *mindscapes*, therefore, just as an anthropologist and a landscape artist must do; she must learn to read them in order to help understand and process the most polarized geographies. And do so while knowing that every map (from the most imaginative ones of antiquity to the satellite images of today) is a historicized object that transmits a personal image of the world.

Inside the landscape, *that* special landscape, we hear the sound of memories we cannot recall. Sometimes we feel as if we're being welcomed, acknowledged, and reborn, and we would like to call *that* place our home in the world. "Wind on the forehead, roar of the sea, light, for hours [...] joy with a sense of gratitude, towards whom?" Fachinelli wonders. His ecstatic mind responds by looking beyond the shore: "Not meditation or recollection. *Acceptance with half-closed eyes.*"[12]

It is the opposite of feeling *displaced*—we feel *set in place*. The landscape, which we see without being seen ourselves, and which—since it exists in itself—can easily do without us, also knows how to contain us. When this happens, it is a therapeutic experience. As I write this, I think that the present-day meaning of the word "therapist"—the person who provides the cure—embraces the ancient meanings of servant and guardian of the temple, of the home, of the place.

Bollas is right: when we start working with a person in analysis, it is as if we were moving to another city. Bit by bit we get to know her culture, her aesthetics, her objects. It's a new landscape, another latitude. Here are its characteristics: the downtown streets, the abandoned areas, the secret corners, a polluted river, some ruins, the cemetery, the factory, the amusement park. The clinical dialogue shows—as in a typical "building cut" by the 1970s photographer and architect Gordon Matta Clark—the intertwining of places, real or imaginary, and psychic functions/functioning: caves for learning how to protect oneself; harbors for stocking up on supplies before going back out to explore the world; towers for looking down from above, and tunnels for descending beneath; markets for exchanging objects; libraries for storing knowledge; virtual spaces for meeting strangers. Like Benjamin's Paris, the session "splits for him into its dialectical poles," "opens up to him as a landscape, even as it closes around him as a room."[13]

For Jung, it was a dream that revealed to him that the human psyche has the structure of a house layered in history:

> I was in a house I did not know, which had two stories. It was "my house." I found myself in the upper story, where there was a kind of salon furnished with fine old pieces in rococo style. [...] Descending the stairs, I reached the ground floor. There everything was much older, and I realized that this part of the house must date from about the fifteenth or sixteenth century. [...] I came upon a heavy door, and opened it. Beyond it, I discovered a stone stairway that led down into the cellar. Descending again, I found myself in a beautifully vaulted room which looked exceedingly ancient. [...] I knew that the walls dated from Roman times. [...] I looked more closely at the floor. It was of stone slabs, and in one of these I discovered a ring. When I pulled it, the stone slab lifted, and again I saw a stairway of narrow stone steps leading down into the depths. These, too, I descended, and entered a low cave cut into the rock. [...] in the dust were scattered

bones and broken pottery, like remains of a primitive culture. I discovered two human skulls, obviously very old and half disintegrated. Then I awoke.[14]

Even language, says Wittgenstein, "can be seen as an ancient city: a maze of little streets and squares, of old and new houses, and of houses with additions from various periods; and this surrounded by a multitude of new boroughs with straight regular streets and uniform houses."[15] This image takes us back to the long Freudian metaphor of the city of Rome as the unconscious, of which I'll offer just this fragment:

Now let us, by a flight of imagination, suppose that Rome is not a human habitation but a psychical entity with a similarly long and copious past—an entity, that is to say, in which nothing that has once come into existence will have passed away and all the earlier phases of development continue to exist alongside the latest one.[16]

If *every city* and *every language* is stratified memory—is a personal and collective unconscious—today we have many unspeakable examples of identity erased, of the physical and psychic devastation brought by a bottomless pit of trauma: Aleppo, Mariupol, Gaza.

A city, a mountaintop, or a sand dune can be looked at or thought about, in different ways, even simultaneously: these are real slices of the world, places of memory, affective markers of our biographies, mirrors of our emotions, elaborations of our imagination, names that resonate.

At the end of the first volume of the *Recherche,* in the part titled "Place-Names: The Name," Proust introduces us to the theme of places, the imaginative intensity that accompanies them, the evocative importance of their names floating around in our memories. In Proust's toponymy, one of the main places is Balbec, a beach near those "mournful coasts, famous for so many shipwrecks, enveloped for six months of the year by the shroud of mists and the foam of waves" where—despite hotels being superimposed on it "without being able to modify the earth's most ancient skeleton"—one can nevertheless sense "the true end of the earth that is French, European, and ancient. And it's the last camp of the fishermen, like all the fishermen who have lived since the beginning of the world, facing the eternal kingdom of sea mists and shadows."[17]

Certain names inhabit our imagination according to our sensibilities. It was Timbuktu for Chatwin, Sana'a for Pasolini, Tangier for Paul Bowles, America for the young Stavros of Elia Kazan's *America, America*. It was Patagonia for Melville, who invented the adjective "Patagonian" to indicate an exotic and fatal attraction ("the attending marvels of a thousand Patagonian sights and sounds, helped to sway me to my wish").[18] Patagonia: Caliban is said to have come from there. Dreams of the other and dreams of elsewhere, metaphors of the extreme, rediscovered paradises, encounters with the unknown, psychic refuges, sensual explorations, aesthetic redemptions, points of no return, "antipodean mirage, a symbol for the back of beyond":[19] the list could be endless.

Is this, as Chatwin would say, literature taking the upper hand over life? Is this restlessness, psychic nomadism, *elsewhere*-o-philia? Is this a way of fantasizing? Is this the idiomatic encounter between mental geographies and geographies in the proper sense—that is, terrestrial geographies? Why do I still cherish the inscription on my passport from 30 years ago, "*Vu au passage a Tombouctou le 7 Janvier 1987,*" written by a Tuareg customs officer?—It's a phrase that sticks with me, even more so now that Timbuktu has been devastated by war and is threatened by terror. The answer is in the line from Pontalis that we started with—to be ourselves, we must contain many places within ourselves[20]—when those "many places" become (as in a psychic condensation, or an obsession) a circumscribed geography, like a dream that repeats itself, or a falling-in-love that does not fade and that disregards the passing of time. We could also call it a form of melancholy, as Baudelaire would say:

> These beautiful and great ships, imperceptibly rocking (swaying) on the quiet waters, these robust ships, with their idle and nostalgic air—do they not say to us in a mute language: When do we depart for happiness?[21]

People generally consider landscape chiefly as an emotional experience, and part of what I have written in this book revolves around that dimension. This does not mean that I think of landscape as a mere projection—aestheticizing and anthropomorphizing—of human states of mind, a position which could be understood as sentimental or hypersubjective;[22] I can't forget that Rilke rebukes anyone who uses landscape as a way of talking about human feelings, thus denying its sublime indifference to us. Rilke's radical and heartbreaking idea is that "the landscape is foreign to us," that among trees and streams we are "frighteningly alone" and that—even in the company of a corpse—we would feel less abandoned than if we were alone in a forest. Only art, he says, can mediate an otherwise illusory encounter with nature. Then a building can evoke the image of a forest and a symphony can contain "the voices of a stormy day" as they merge "with the murmur of our blood."[23] The meaning of this image from Rilke is clear to anyone who has visited Mahler's composing huts in Klagenfurt am Wörthersee or in Toblach and listened to his *Song of the Earth* (*Das Lied von der Erde*).

It would be animism to deny the indifference in which the landscape is immersed and to instead attribute a mind to it. Humanizing it or anthropizing it means denying its otherness, transforming it into a domesticated mirror. Our relationship with the landscape cannot be reduced to a complacent surrender to postcard-like sunsets or to escapes into Caribbean screen-saver photos during our workdays. Experiencing the landscape, experiencing its mythical power, brings us to a sense of sacrality (sometimes due precisely to the otherness of nature, and its "indifference" to us). Disappearing into the landscape, forgetting oneself, and attenuating one's egocentrism are always healing experiences.

"Landscape is nature that reveals itself aesthetically to those who observe and contemplate it with feeling":[24] while Ritter's classic definition (which excludes from the landscape cultivated fields, bridges and rivers used as borders, steppes with shepherds and caravans) has been useful to all studies of the landscape, it's still the case that landscape is not just the vision of beauty. To look at a place without the lenses of memory and of culture, stripping it of the artistic heritage that has grown up in its spaces, would be to deny the link between the human and the non-human environment. It would be to deny the existence, for good or evil (caused or received), of an interdependence. The identity of a place is also the result of the gaze that has rested on it and, often, the result of human labor. Allowing an identification and promoting an identification, they in turn provide an identity.

According to the *European Landscape Convention*, landscape is not "a purely objective phenomenon (such as the territory or the environment) nor purely subjective (the infamous landscape as a state of mind)," but something that is constituted "in the interaction between the two sides." It is not only a "co-presence of natural and historical elements, cultural and physical-biological elements," but above all a "resource of

identity."[25] It is the sense of connection with the non-human environment of which Searles speaks, and it constitutes one of the psychologically relevant aspects of our lives.

The relationship with the landscape is far more eventful than mere
projection, and more varied than mere subjectification. Landscape
reflects our feelings but it also prompts our feelings. We could say that we
"use" the landscape and its parts as objects for the discovery and the
elaboration of our psychic life, as a "holding" function that's necessary
for our development. Of course, I say "use" in Winnicott's sense of the
word, gesturing to the ability to play; not contemplating exploitation,
but implying the possibility of experiencing negative feelings. The impossibility or inability to "use" the landscape can produce a disharmony
between the self and the object, and can lead to a type of depressive
condition that Bollas calls "aesthetic dejection."[26]

Our relationship to the landscape is less unidirectional than we think.
The landscape is not merely sitting there to receive projections of our feelings. It helps us rediscover memories and sensations, perceive corporeity,
to reveal new thoughts: these are experiences induced by the landscape
when it acts on us (and not vice versa). Crossroads of psychic and real
objects, perceptions and representations: we can immerse ourselves in the
landscape as if it were a semi-dreamlike product. Meltzer used to say that
dreams were his landscape.[27] But how many landscapes are in dreams!

Notes

1 Pier Paolo Pasolini. *A Bertolucci [For Bertolucci]* from *Nuovi Epigrammi
   (1958–59) [New Epigrams (1958–59)]* in *La Religione del Mio Tempo [The
   Religion of My Time]* © Garzanti Editore s.p.a., 1961, 1976, 1995; © 1999,
   2001, 2005, 2010, Garzanti S.r.l., Milan. Gruppo editoriale Mauri Spagnol.
2 Bachelard, Gaston. *The Poetics of Space*. Translated by Maria Jolas, copyright © 1958 by Presses Universitaires de France. Translation copyright ©
   1964 by Penguin Random House LLC.
3 Osbourne, Lawrence. *The Naked Tourist. In Search of Adventure and Beauty
   in the Age of the Airport Mall*. New York: North Pole Press, 2006.
4 Schorske, Carl. *Fin-De-Siecle Vienna: Politics and Culture*. New York:
   Alfred A. Knopf, 1980.
5 Roudinesco, Élisabeth. *Freud: In His Time and Ours*. Cambridge, MA:
   Harvard University Press, 2016.
6 Freud, Sigmund. *The Origins of Psychoanalysis. Sigmund Freud's Letters*.
   Translated by Eric Mosbacher and James Strachey. New York: Basic Books,
   1954, p. 236.

7 Musatti's words from his preface to Volume 4 of the Italian edition of the complete works of Freud: Musatti, C. L. Preface to *Sigmund Freud, Opere: Tre saggi sulla teoria sessuale e altri scritti, Vol. 4, 1900–1905 [Sigmund Freud, Works: Three Essays on Sexual Theory and Other Writings, Vol. 4, 1900–1905]*. Turin: Bollati Boringhieri, 1977.

8 Freud, Sigmund. *Il nostro cuore volge al Sud. Lettere di viaggio. Soprattutto dall'Italia [Our Heart Points to the South: Travel Letters. 1895–1923]*. Milan: Bompiani, 2003.

9 Roudinesco, Élisabeth. "I viaggi di Freud [Freud's Travels]." Italian translation. *Lettera internazionale*, 89 (2006), p. 3.

10 Jones, Ernest. *Sigmund Freud: Life and Work. Vol 2: The Years of Maturity 1901–1919*. London: Hogarth Press, 1955.

11 "A Disturbance of Memory on the Acropolis," in *The Standard Edition of the Complete Psychological Works of Sigmund Freud, Vol. XXII (1932–36)*. Translated by James Strachey. London: The Hogarth Press, 1964.

12 Fachinelli, Elvio. *La mente estatica [The Ecstatic Mind]*. Milan: Adelphi, 1989. The italics are mine.

13 Benjamin, Walter. *The Arcades Project*. Translated by Rolf Tiedemann. New York: The Belknap Press of Harvard University Press, 1999.

14 Jung, Carl Gustav. *Memories, Dreams, Reflections*. New York: Vintage, 2011.

15 Wittgenstein, Ludwig. *Philosophical Investigations*. Translated by G. E. M. Anscombe. New York: Wiley-Blackwell, 2009.

16 Freud, Sigmund. *Civilization and Its Discontents*, in *The Standard Edition of the Complete Psychological Works of Sigmund Freud*. London: Hogarth Press and the Institute of Psycho-Analysis, 1953 [1930].

17 Proust, Marcel. *À la recherche du temps perdu: Du côté de chez Swann [In Search of Lost Time: Swann's Way]*, 1913. Balbec is a fictional town in Normandy based on the real-life town of Cabourg.

18 Melville, Herman. *Moby Dick*, 1851.

19 Chatwin, Bruce. "Gone to Timbuctoo," in *Anatomy of Restlessness. Selected Writings 1969–1989*. New York: Viking, 1996.

20 Pontalis, Jean-Bertrand. *L'amour des commencements [Love of Beginnings]*. Paris: Gallimard, 1986.

21 Baudelaire, Charles. *Journaux Intimes: Mon Cœur Mis a Nu [Intimate Journals: My Heart Laid Bare]*, 1887.

22 See D'Angelo, Paolo (ed.), *Estetica e paesaggio [Aesthetics and Landscape]*. Bologna: Il Mulino, 2009; and Carchia, Gianni. "Per una filosofia del paesaggio [Philosophy of Landscape]," *Quaderni di Estetica e Critica* 4–5 (1999–2000), pp. 13–21.

23 Rilke, Rainer Maria. *Worpswede [Worpswede]*. Italian translation. Milan: Claudio Gallone, 1998.

24 Ritter, Joachim. *Paesaggio. Uomo e natura nell'età moderna [Landscape. Man and Nature in the Modern Age.]*. Translated by G. Catalano. Milan: Guerini e Associati, 2001.

25 D'Angelo, Paolo (ed.). *Estetica e paesaggio [Aesthetics and Landscape]*. Bologna: il Mulino, 2009, p. 35.

26 Bollas, Christopher. *The Evocative Object World*. New York: Routledge, 2009, p. 57.

27 Meltzer, Donald (unpublished letter), quoted in Harris Williams, Meg. *The Aesthetic Development. The Poetic Spirit of Psychoanalysis*. New York: Karnac, 2010.

Chapter 8

Close your eyes and you'll see

Only landscapes already seen in dreams are observed with aesthetic passion.

Gaston Bachelard, *Psychoanalysis of the Waters*[1]

With cities, it is as with dreams: everything imaginable can be dreamed, but even the most unexpected dream is a rebus that conceals a desire or, its reverse, a fear. Cities, like dreams, are made of desires and fears, even if the thread of their discourse is secret, their rules are absurd, their perspectives deceitful, and everything conceals something else.

Italo Calvino, *Invisible Cities*[2]

Each of us has our own view of the origin and meaning of dreams. For the ancients, dreams were a manifestation of divine will. Soothsayers and priests read meanings by plucking out the signals that would determine the (auspicious or inauspicious) course of events. The disposition to interpret dreams, to grasp and unveil their hidden meanings, is common to all eras—but it is only with Freud's *Interpretation of Dreams*, published as the 1800s became the 1900s, that dreams got ferried into the new century.

Flectere si nequeo Superos, Acheronta movebo: "If I cannot bend the supreme gods, I will move the Acheron." Virgil's words, chosen by Freud as his epigraph, seem to emphasize the transition from the dream as an expression (Superos) to the dream as a production of the deep psyche (Acheronta). Speaking of the "dream scene," Freud evokes the

DOI: 10.4324/9781003252979-8

idea of a "psychic locality," not determined "in an anatomical sense," but recognized "on the psychological terrain" as a point "in which one of the preliminary stages of the image is formed." Geography and vision appear together on the oneiric scene. The Freudian unconscious is a subsoil,[3] a realm of Hades pregnant with waters and with urges. Weren't there five rivers running through the classical Underworld? The Styx, river of hatred, was one; another was the Acheron, river of affliction; and then came the Cocytus, the river of lamentation; the Phlegethon, the river of fire; and the Lethe, river of oblivion. After all, sleep brings us devils and fiends, as depicted in Johann Heinrich Füssli's *Nightmare* and Francisco Goya's *The Sleep of Reason Produces Monsters*.

When we read that Jung noted that "the fear and resistance that every natural man feels when he digs too deep into himself are, in the last analysis, the fear of the journey into Hades,"[4] we have all the ingredients to understand Gustave Doré's engraving of *Charon* (in his illustration for the *Divine Comedy*) and to understand why all *psychologies of the profound* eventually bring the waters and caverns and oneiric fogs back to "natural" landscapes of the unconscious.

But if dreams are immersed in the infernal landscape, in the *depths*, an analyst tends to think that his task is to bring "up" to the *surface*, what lies "below." *Fiat lux*—let there be light. This is indeed partly the case, but interpretation is not always the appropriate tool. Although Freud considered interpretation as a translation "into the language of the vigilant life,"[5] analytic work on dreams is not a "simple" work of translation from one language to another. On the contrary—given that a dream narrative is already a translation (with many elements lost in translation)—we might as well "look at the figures." Like a landscape, a dream demands vision and sensory immersion, aesthetic attention and imagination. Not necessarily to embrace the *mundus imaginalis* beloved by Corbin[6] and taken up by Hillman as well: sure, that has its appeal, but it also has its danger, like anything esoteric. Especially in the analyst's office, which is not a Sufi gymnasium.

The keywords of analytical psychology, *image* and *imaginative act*, are in Jung's view the basis of "every psychic event": without them, there could be no consciousness at all.[7] The concept of image, Jung explains, comes "from poetic language" and does not mean "psychic reproduction of the external object," but rather "fantastic image," a condensed expression of the total psychic situation, which can only indirectly be referred to the perception of the external object.[8] The image appears suddenly to the consciousness, like "a vision" or "a hallucination," without being pathological. It can be a personal or a primordial image (that is: archetypal, archaic, common to a culture or to an era). As for dreams, Jung strongly doubts that they can be seen "as something other than what they appear" and, contrary to Freud, he prefers to take a dream "for what it is." The plot of a dream, he says, is "so obscure and intricate that I dare not formulate an opinion about its possible innate tendency to deception." "We must use a great deal of prudence," he concludes, "in introducing into the explanation elements foreign to the dream itself."[9]

Right now, I do not want to venture to compare different psychoanalytic approaches to dreams—this is not an academic treatise. Among other things, I would risk getting sucked into landscapes of another kind: psychodynamic models. Although Jung said, with ironic irreverence, that on the subject of dreams he preferred to quote another Jewish authority, the Talmud, "where it is said that 'the dream *is* its own interpretation,'"[10] still I believe that a dream *has* the interpretation of the person who *dreams* it (so much so that there is a literature on the possible different interpretations of the same dream—Freudian, Jungian, Kleinian, Bionian, Lacanian). Since *mindscapes* are (also) visual landscapes, the excursions that I have allowed myself in this chapter have been in the Jungian field and in the Bionian field. Each in its own way favors the visual-sensory dimensions of oneiric activity—and therefore of our psychic life.

More than a century has passed since *The Interpretation of Dreams*, and psychoanalysis is much changed. Freud's vision of man as an animal governed by drives has given way to a vision of the human being as a subject that generates a meaning that is constructed in relationships. New ways of imagining the unconscious, and a (justified) pull toward delocalizing it, lead us to talk about unconscious processes, radically rethinking the dream experience. These days, psychoanalysis—after having laid aside most of the interpretative armamentarium—often in dialogue with neuroscience, looks at dreams not as encrypted material to be *revealed* but as a visual neuro-laboratory to be *recounted*. The dream can be considered a form of thought, a capacity of the mind to create images and stories of our psychic life, to represent emotional states, consolidate memories, metabolize emotions and sensations, connect states of the self, relate to other people, formulate aesthetic experiences, and even solve problems.

It appears that the right hemisphere plays a crucial role in dream production, and we know that its activation is linked to imaginative, creative, and artistic dimensions.[11] The point of contact between Bion and Schnitzler, two great enthusiasts of the dream, might be exactly this: the oneiric unconscious (which, as we will see, works during sleep and during wakefulness) is the workshop in which life and its narration are produced simultaneously. The unconscious, once a *place*, becomes a *function*. Once a *warehouse*, it becomes a *laboratory*.

Dreams, which elude us while they also sustain us, sow stories and images in the fields of the psyche—stories that accompany us throughout our lives. Even if dreams are just random neurological material, an epiphenomenon of sleep that is itself insignificant,[12] or the consequence of a heavy dinner or the buzzing of a bee, dreams would still represent an involuntary narrative, an autobiographical thread, a welling-up of memories and objects, a bridge towards what we do not know, a mental landscape. Such a dream can cause a surrealist nightmare—as in Salvador Dalí's painting, *Dream Caused by the Flight of a Bee Around a Pomegranate a Second Before Awakening*.

When we dream, we are immersed in the landscape. Dream landscapes have a particular evocative power—whether for their ability to manifest in unconventional ways, or for the immediacy with which they manage to express the relationship between the internal world and external reality. In clinical practice and in the dream experience, we frequently note the intertwining of dreamscapes, emotional states, and biographical events. A dream, we might say, is an extreme form of mindscape.

In his dream diary, begun in 1875 and finished in 1931, Schnitzler noted how sometimes in a dream nature will show itself in poignantly precise shapes which are unattainable in waking life and perceived in sleep with intense purity. It is not the mechanism of memory that stops and transfigures the perceived world, says Schnitzler; it is the absolute clarity of the image caught in the dreamlike present:

Dream of February 21, 1900: With P. M. Spring landscape, Rodaun, French forest. Springtime and a green of unprecedented beauty—as seen only in a dream. A terrible pain assails me that the Disappeared One can no longer see all this, and, crying loudly, I wake up.[13]

Strange landscapes punctuate our oneiric repertoire: "I'm at the seaside, but there's snow," "I'm crossing the garden of my father's house, but my feet are sinking into the grass as if I were in quicksand." Likewise, narrative figures in our dreams evoke daring cognitive or perceptual operations ("it was my mother, but also my sister," "the head was that of a cat, but the body was that of a child") and that follow syntax and rhetoric noted way back by Freud: condensations, displacements, symbolizations, deformations, inversions, and so on.

One of my patients dreams of her house as a "vertical forest," referring explicitly to the Milanese skyscraper of leafy balconies designed by Stefano Boeri. In the course of her analysis, the expression "vertical forest" will become a synonym, for us, of her attempt to give roots and affective vegetation to her ambitious intellectual drives. This image will be enriched by her childhood memories and emotions: her father the industrialist, a successful man who was always traveling for business; her melancholy mother, off in the countryside with her daughter, spending time together in the vegetable garden.

Geographies recur in the analysis sessions. Notions both real and imaginary, sometimes anchored in common knowledge of people and countries, these geographies express—in dreams or free associations—our patients' inclinations, fears, and desires. Francesca dreams of cultivating a desert. Luigi dreams of climbing a mountain whose peak he cannot see. Giovanni dreams of being embraced by Balkan kids, because "they are stronger than Italian kids, more cunning—and they have a story to tell."

In Lucia's dreams, spaces are primordial, "Patagonian": great deserts and oceans and glaciers where she is a very small figure and she can hardly see herself. Louis introduces himself in a botanical way, like this: "I am a cactus; I need watering only once a month," he says, and a few sessions later I grasp what he was telling me, when he won't even consider my proposal to see each other twice a week.

Mountain/sea. North/south. Cold/warm. Clothed/naked. Open eyes/closed eyes. Polarized geographies, oppositions. Anna and Marco, who have been married for 20 years, have a tried and tested matrimonial rule, which they consider to be a fundamental ingredient of their marriage's success. At vacation time, Anna, who "needs" the mountains ("fresh air and thin air, rocks and meadows"), joins her rock-climber friends in the Alps. Marco, who "needs" the sea ("warm air and salt air, being naked, sand and flip-flops"), goes to Sicily with his daughter. Anna wants to *climb* (sharp peaks, oceans of snow, silence, emptiness, the experience of the sublime, *sub-limen*: reaching almost all the way to the highest limit). Marco wants to *descend* ("the sea air will burn my lungs; the remote climates will tan me. Swimming, treading on the grass…").[14] Anna knows that "winter is an abstract season" and that "at low temperatures beauty is beauty."[15] Marco hates winter: "Because winter hates flesh. Wherever it discovers flesh, it punishes it, lashing it like a puritanical preacher."[16]

Like Aida and Radamès, Anna and Marco counterpose their two different geographies against one another. Then they devote a second part of their vacation to a journey that they choose together; each year they strive to reconcile Marco's pull southward and Anna's pull to the north. In time they will find each other again, learning to move within each other's *mindscapes* as well. As Wallace Stevens would say, North and South are a tightly bound couple.[17]

To illustrate the concept of "unformulated experience," Donnel Stern uses a dream.[18] The dream is interesting because it illuminates the dreamlike experience of landscape as psychic content. The dreamer is a 30-year-old man, recently divorced, who feels so sad and distressed that he can barely imagine the future. In the dream he is driving on an icy, winding mountain road. Snow is falling heavily. A great silence reigns; the landscape is motionless under a grey blanket of clouds. Unexpectedly, around a bend, the sun appears and the driver/patient is struck by the mountain-tops glittering against the blue sky. Further down is a large forest with green trees. Well-being and satisfaction suddenly wash over him. After listening to the patient's associations, Stern shares with him the idea that the dream might be a way in which his psyche is sketching out the internal resources—hitherto unimagined, but probably available—for building a new landscape after his long depressive curve. Of course, the same landscape, at a different moment, for a different patient, could lead us to the opposite idea: glittering peaks and verdant forests could also imply that, beyond the depressive curve, a manic surge is lurking.

The landscape not only furnishes the context for our dreams that permit individuation or give voice to experiences that are not yet formulated, but it also appears in nightmares, with catastrophic or polluted images that show the oneiric translation of psychic suffering. I will never forget a dream reported by Ariadne, a 15-year-old who had attempted suicide four times:

> I'm with my family in our beach house. Everyone is sleeping; I am awake and I decide to open the window—maybe I want to jump out, or maybe just watch the sunrise. I don't know. I open the shutters and the sea is gone. In its place is an immense garbage dump. It's as if the sea had receded, leaving only the debris of the sea-floor.

"I dream that I'm in the mountains," Massimo tells me; he's an engineer in his thirties, a skilled skier, and his fear of contracting sexually transmitted diseases, even just from kissing, has paralyzed his emotional life and his ability to feel pleasure. "It's a beautiful day. I decide to take off my skis and soak up the sun. I stick my skis into the snow, unbutton my shirt, and spread my jacket out so I can sit down. After a while I realize that the snow is, like, radioactive: it's melting the windbreaker and corroding my skis. I realize that I have become contaminated and that nothing can be done."

Mario is an educated physician who feels that ever since childhood he's had some basic shortcoming, a structural lack that makes him weak, vulnerable, and solitary. So he must always be ready to respond to attacks from an enemy—from a colleague or a neighbor. "I can't get into a relationship," he says. "My army is too busy defending my borders from possible attack; every resource is committed to making me look normal." He prefers the pain of loneliness over the uncertainty of sharing. He feels inhabited by a recurring image. "Sometimes it's a pictorial dream," he says,

> sometimes it's a kind of inner vision, that's present even when I'm awake. Can you picture one of those de Chirico landscapes? That's how I feel—I *see* myself like that: mannequins, metaphysical architecture, no human presence. On the horizon is a train, which I will never ride. And sometimes I *see* myself as a Sironi painting instead: dark buildings, black skies, solid bodies without windows.

Rossella is just over 40 years old. It is likely that as a child she was abused by her father. She is ashamed of herself, she is childish, she seems unintelligent. In the sessions she is "superficial." After two years of sessions—a continuous relationship, but with stunted conversations accompanied by (probably post-traumatic) dream-images to which she cannot attach any stories—"a little girl in a coffin," "a withered rose," "a handkerchief dirty with phlegm," "the erect penis of a dog"—something begins to change. Her emotional and analytical awakening is accompanied by a dream that is "narrated," for once:

I find myself in a landscape that is like Dante's *Purgatory*, foggy. I put on my mask and go into the sea. I see hippos embedded in the rocks, but when I look again, I see that they are not hippos, but donkeys that bray and cry a lot. I start to ask how long they've been stuck down there, and I hear a voice say: 40 years.

Her snorkeling mask allows her to see parts of her Self that are stuck, stranded. The outside world is still foggy; it is a limbo of "those souls who are suspended" (as Dante had it), still needing to atone for their faults while looking ahead to a better life. Her dreamlike thought bespeaks a psychic block that has lasted 40 years (Rossella started analysis at age 40). The dream associations permit undervalued images of herself to surface: the hippos remind her of herself, once a bulimic and clumsy child and now a fat and awkward woman, with friends who probably laugh at her. The donkey is the failing schoolgirl of the past and the inadequate woman of today. The two animals seem to be images of Rossella's self as a child, in tears and imprisoned "down below." Now, however, instead of a coffin that contains a dead girl, there is a rock that contains suffering animals. The living fossils start to melt into tears.

The FRED Group in Frankfurt (FRED stands for Frankfurt fMRI/ EEG Depression Study) has for years been studying the dreams of a group of patients undergoing psychotherapy. By comparing the dreams at the beginning of the treatment with dreams that came after three years of analysis, they have found that persons whose therapy went well also had a significant "improvement" of some dream variables—for example, atmospheres and relational patterns; the range of actions performed; the breadth of the emotional spectrum. Other research has been devoted to identifying specific features of the dream life of traumatized patients; for example, while the subjects in the control group dreamed without awakening, those in the experimental group—when a dream presented a traumatic theme—woke up distressed: probably they were unable to metabolize the dream contents during their sleep.[19] On the other hand, every clinician knows that night terrors—and also flashbacks and involuntary memories—are typical for individuals suffering from post-traumatic stress disorder (even many years later). And every clinician knows that recovering the ability to dream is an indicator that therapy is working.

Although it is an intimate and personal event, a dream does not constitute a separate world and it does not occur outside of time. When times are tough—when a whole community is collectively going through a difficult period—dreams unite our thoughts and concerns, and thus our unconscious. In 1936, when Hitler seized power, German journalist Charlotte Beradt solicited dream reports from her acquaintances; the dreams were full of anguish and dread, and years later (in 1966) she published them in a book titled *The Third Reich of Dreams*.[20] These diaries of the night, she wrote, were partly independent of the dreamer's consciousness. They were "dictated by dictatorship." Indeed, certain themes recur: mind control, surprise searches, the imposition of rules, the loss of individuality. Decades later, researchers Ernest Hartmann and Tyler Brezler[21] analyzed dreams from 44 people, each of whom provided ten dreams they had had after the attacks of September 11, 2001, and ten dreams from before the traumatic event. The goal in reviewing these 880 dreams was to assess any changes produced on the "Central Image of the dream," defined as a dream image that is distinguished by its power and vividness. One interesting finding from this research is that the prevailing image of post-attack dreams was not directly related to the attack on the Twin Towers—but the concept of being attacked increased sharply, transposed (in some cases) into scenes of normal daily life. The dreams represented worry and distress, without necessarily replicating the images of the attack. Starting in 2020, I did a study on dreams from during the Covid-19 pandemic lockdown.[22] From hundreds of reports, I tried to construct a community dream narrative, searching for common themes and testing the idea that the unconscious is a collective laboratory as well as an individual laboratory, where each person's unique story dwells but where we can also hear echoes of events that grip the whole world. This dream map has nothing to do with interpretation and even less to do with therapy: it is simply a way to collect and systematize the themes of a collective dreaming, perhaps a way to process the unexpected traumatic event of a virus that changed everyone's life.

Some of these "lockdown dreams" were freighted with a distressing, persecutory, invasive atmosphere; others evoked refuge and protection; still others were encounters with memory: childhood, parents when they were young, friends and partners from past lives.

As clinicians know, post-traumatic moments set the dream world alight: in acute forms (nightmares) or in subtly disturbing atmospheres. Hartmann and Brezler reported that—after the attack on the Twin Towers—the dreams they investigated showed increased intensity of "Central Images" with emotional content; for example, "I was being swept away by a giant wave." Similarly, in the lockdown dreams in my study, water was a recurring image—in the form of a flood or tsunami. Although water often appears in dreams in a million unclassifiable ways, here the recurring image of the tsunami (imprinted on our group memory since the Indian Ocean earthquake/tsunami of December 26, 2004) seemed to evoke the terror of a collective traumatic event—that overwhelming residue that Philip Bromberg calls "the shadow of the tsunami."[23] Contagion was another recurrent theme: contamination in various forms, accompanied sometimes by anguish, and sometimes by the capacity to cope with the threat, or to brilliantly overcome the terror. The contagious figures were mostly animals, but also objects and people. Here are some examples (brief excerpts, to save space here): "a pen bursts on my face, creating indelible ink stains despite repeated washing with soap and water"; "a white mouse/bat comes into my kitchen and goes to the refrigerator for food"; "in a crowd… people are shoving us… I get all scratched up and then I realize that what looks like a scratch is actually a needle stuck into my skin"; "a moldy wall, swollen with water… teeming with alien life, pulsing—it's reddish… big leeches along the walls"; "I kissed a friend on the cheek. But no!—what did I do? How could I have been so foolish? I run to the bathroom. I disinfect everything—cheeks and lips—with antibacterial soap and warm water. I curse myself. I prepare myself psychologically to see the symptoms begin." Another recurring theme was separation: separation as loneliness, misunderstanding, isolation, physical or emotional distance. And then there were dreams that "enacted" the pandemic, the archetypal fantasy of pestilence as a theater of death and apocalypse. Two examples: "I was walking among a herd of dead cows, white, piled atop one another; other cows were alive, brown, and looking at me"; "I am at home and watching from the window as the world is crumbling, the earth cracks, people are swallowed up by rivers of earth and debris." Lastly, some dreams were comforting, compensatory: a sense of shelter, a childhood home, memory, nature in its mercy. "I am by the sea, I feel the wind on my face... my parents [who are actually dead] are healthy and younger." But what most surprised me was the frequency (at least in our sample) of dreams of motherhood. Come to think of it, we should have expected this: doesn't the desire for life get even stronger in a deadly time? These were dreams of women surprised by a pregnancy—worried, protective, wild: epiphanies of rebirth, gifts of the female unconscious that grasps the secrets of life and death better than anyone else.

Dreaming is an unavoidable activity, like thinking. Imagine how many answers we could give in response to the question "why do we think?" And why separate the activity of thinking from the activity of dreaming? Why not consider the thinking aspects of dreaming, and the dreaming aspects of thinking? Analysis sessions are "*Conversations at the Frontier of Dreaming*" (to cite a book title)[24]—they are a permeable frontier, traversed by nocturnal and diurnal pathways, hallucinatory traces and conscious thoughts, sensory elements and daydreams. A "dream is less a comment on the day," Hillman writes, "than a digestive process of it, a breakdown and assimilation of the dayworld within the labyrinthine tracts of the psyche." This dream-work—to use Hillman's favorite Freudian expression—"cooks life events into psychic substance by means of imaginative modes."[25]

Without getting too hung up on deciphering, Ferro says, patients' dreams "can be grabbed" as they travel on shuttles to the unconscious, shuttles that travel through our *rêveries*. In this sense the analyst is like the poet who captures his or her verses: "thought-foxes"[26] that allow themselves to be glimpsed, for a moment, in the darkness of the forest. After all, a dream, like a poem, "is composed in a wrong, absurd way, and yet absurd and yet very right," and for this reason—like Shakespeare— it creates its own language and a world that is "wholly peculiar."[27]

The dream-work we know is only a small aspect of dreaming proper— dreaming proper being a continuous process belonging to the *waking* life in action all through the waking hours, but not usually observable then except with the psychotic patient.[28]

It used to be a one-way trip from consciousness to dreaming. With the advent of Bionian psychoanalysis (and with echoes of Shakespeare and Calderón de la Barca) the oneiric has been expanded: a dream is no longer an exclusively nocturnal phenomenon, it is also a waking activity, a function which transforms into images the swarm of stimuli and sensations that tirelessly affects us. Bion calls it "alpha function," i.e., transformation of the "beta elements" (raw sensory and emotional data, "indigestible facts," "things in themselves") into "alpha elements" that allow the formation of oneiric thoughts; therefore they are the famous substance of which dreams are made.

The alpha function is thus a filter on the border between consciousness and unconsciousness, a filter without which we could neither be awake, nor asleep, nor think, nor dream.[29] Dream activity allows us to transform and to "aesthetically" represent the stimuli of emotional experience and thus allows us to live, think, and recall those stimuli. A dream is nothing more than a "pictographic representation," verbally expressed, of what has happened. We do not know, says Bion, what we have really "dreamed"; but since we cannot tolerate the unknown, we instantly strive to feel that it is explainable and familiar.[30] The alpha function allows us to "digest" reality and form representations of "things." Without it, the psyche becomes psychosis.

While Freud considered dreaming to be a way of protecting the ego from the overwhelming forces of the unconscious, accumulated underground, Bion considered dreaming to be a way of protecting the unconscious from the overwhelming irruption of external stimuli.[31] Without our realizing it, our sensations, perceptions, and emotions—or rather proto-emotions—are alphabetized,[32] transformed into words, visual matrices, pictograms. Dream activity becomes a "visual poetry of the psychic apparatus"[33] that comes to life again during the session as an exchange of images between patient and analyst. Dreams as "forest glades" (again in Zambrano's term)? I am impressed but not surprised when I see her affirm (almost as if she is speaking Bion's language), that "dreams do not manifest themselves only while one is asleep: they also appear in the waking state, staining it, perforating it."[34]

Listening to dreams, sharing them, paying attention to their language, their style, and their emotional climate—including the awakening—are attitudes (analytical and otherwise) that provide important information about psychic functioning. The Freudian analyst inside us can dwell on the dream's content; the Jungian analyst can dwell on the dream's journey; the Bionian one can dwell on transformation; the Lacanian one on language. And each one can capture the relational dynamics (past and present) that the dream brings with it, including the intersubjective exchange with the analyst who listens and participates. We can, like

Fonagy, consider the dream as an attempt at pre-reflexive mental self-representation, the litmus test not only of the internal theater, but also of the ability to represent it. The oneiric event is also a window on the narrative competence of the dreamer's unconscious. When we work with traumatized patients, we realize that dreams can function as a reservoir of implicit memory, becoming, when words are missing—and not because they are silent or repressed, but because they are yet to be known—an involuntary and privileged channel of analytical communication.[35] The mysterious synaptic interweaving from which the dream originates—thoughts, visions, perceptions, memories—can start threads of memories and ideas for the future. Scanty dreaming and dream strangeness may indicate difficulties in mental functioning. One function of the analyst, Ogden reminds us, is to help the patient dream the dreams he has not dreamed—or has been unable to dream. In the multiplicity of states of the self that Bromberg hypothesized, *oneiric reality* is nothing more than a different state of consciousness (but it's not out of reach: "the dissociative gap between a sleep state and a waking state is as permeable as the space between any two states").[36]

Taking notes in anticipation of a novel, Schnitzler spoke of seeing moving images unspooling before his eyes. As in a dream, a *Double Dream*, the beta elements are transformed into imaginative narratives and the analyst's study becomes a field of joint narratives, suspended between historical truth and clinical truth, reconstruction and relation. A here and now in continuous transformative oscillation with a there and then.

"Before being a conscious vision, every landscape is a dreamlike vision."[37] Bachelard's hyperbole makes me think that the landscape we love is something we have already dreamed. That we can look at landscape as if it were a dream and look at a dream as if it were a landscape. Both allow us to—like an artist—arrange real objects on the psychic scene. Both of them love to be explored, but they suffer from our intrusiveness. Dreams should be treated as "a work of art," says Jung,[38] with restraint and delicacy, and "taking nuance into account."

Notes

1 Bachelard, Gaston. *On Poetic Imagination and Reverie: Selections from the Works of Gaston Bachelard*. Trans. Colette Gaudin. New York: Spring Publications, 1998, p. 36.

2 Calvino, Italo. *Invisible Cities*. Translated by William Weaver. San Diego: Harcourt Brace & Company, 1974, p. 44. *Le città invisibili* copyright © 1972 by Giulio Einaudi Editore, used by permission of The Wylie Agency LLC. English translation copyright © 1974 by Harcourt, Inc. Used by permission of HarperCollins Publishers.

3 Hillman, James. *The Dream and the Underworld*. New York: Harper & Row, 1979.

4 Jung, Carl. *Psicologia e alchimia [Psychology and Alchemy]*. Italian translation in *Opere*, Vol. 12. Turin: Boringhieri, 1992.

5 Freud, Sigmund. "Symbolism in Dreams," in *The Standard Edition of the Complete Psychological Works*, Vols. 1–24. London: The Hogarth Press and the Institute of Psychoanalysis, 1953–1974.

6 Henry, Corbin (1903–1978), a French philosopher and Orientalist, looked to the Arab philosopher, mystic, and poet Ibn' Arabi (1165–1240) for the concept of creative imagination of the heart, which is condensed in the Arabic word himma, i.e., the creative power of the heart. See also Hillman, James. *The Dream and the Underworld*. New York: Harper & Row, 1979.

7 Jung, Carl. "Prefazione a D. T. Suzuki, La grande liberazione. Introduzione al buddhismo zen." Italian translation in *Opere*, Vol. 11. Turin: Boringhieri, 1979.

8 Jung, Carl. *Tipi psicologici [Psychological Types]*. Italian translation in *Opere*, Vol. 6. Turin: Boringhieri, 1969.

9 Jung, Carl. *Psicologia e religione [Psychology & Religion]*. Italian translation in *Opere*, Vol. 11. Turin: Boringhieri, 1979.

10 Jung, Carl. *Psicologia e religione [Psychology & Religion]*. Italian translation in *Opere*, Vol. 11. Turin: Boringhieri, 1979.

11 Schore, A. *The Science of the Art of Psychotherapy*. Norton: New York, 2012.

12 Many researchers say that—just as we can confirm the existence of waking consciousness—we can speak of sleep-consciousness and dream-consciousness. See for example, Nir, Y., & Tononi, G. "Dreaming and the brain: from phenomenology to neurophysiology," *Trends in Cognitive Sciences* 14, no. 2 (2010), pp. 88–100; and Siclari F., Baird B., Perogamvros L., et al. "The neural correlates of dreaming," *Nature Neuroscience* 20, no. 6 (2017), pp. 872–878.

13 This is a reference to Marie Reinhard, his lover who had borne him a still-born child and who had herself died two years later. In Schnitzler, Arthur, *Sogni (1875–1931) [Dream Story]*. Italian translation. Milan: Il Saggiatore, 2018, p. 18.

14 Rimbaud, Arthur. *Una stagione in inferno [A Season in Hell]*. Italian translation in *Opere*. Milan: Mondadori, 1975, pp. 209–281.

15 Brodsky, Joseph. *Fondamenta degli incurabili [Watermark]*. Italian translation. Milan: Adelphi, 1991.

16 Tournier, Michel. *Il re degli ontani [The Erl-King]*. Italian translation. Milan: Garzanti, 1996.

17 Stevens, Wallace. "Notes Toward a Supreme Fiction," in *Collected Poems*. London: Faber, 2006.

18 Stern, Donnel B. *Unformulated Experience. From Dissociation to Imagination in Psychoanalysis*. Hillsdale, NJ: The Analytic Press, 2003.

19 Fischmann, T., Russ, M. O., and Leuzinger-bohleber, M. "Trauma, dream, and psychic change in psychoanalyses: A dialogue between psychoanalysis and the neurosciences," *Frontiers in Human Neuroscience*, 7 (2013), p. 877. Varvin, S., Fischmann, T., Jovic, V., Rosenbaum, B., and Hau, S. "Traumatic dreams: Symbolisation gone astray," in *The Significance of Dreams, Bridging Clinical and Extraclinical Research in Psychoanalysis*, edited by P. Fonagy, H. Kächele, M. Leuzinger-Bohleber, and D. Taylor. London: Karnac Books, 2012.

20 Beradt, Charlotte. *The Third Reich of Dreams: The Nightmares of a Nation, 1933–1939*. London: Aquarian Press, 1985.

21 Hartmann, E., and Brezler, T. "A systematic change in dreams after 9/11/01." *Sleep* 31, no. 2 (2008), pp. 213–218. Doi: 10.1093/sleep/31.2.213.

22 Giovanardi, G., Bincoletto, A. F., Baiocco, R., Ferrari, M., Gentile, D., Siri, M., Tanzilli, A., Lingiardi, V. "Lockdown dreams: Dream content and emotions during the Covid-19 pandemic in an Italian sample." *Psychoanalytic Psychology* 39, no. 2 (2021), pp. 111–126.

23 Bromberg, Philip M. *The Shadow of the Tsunami: and the Growth of the Relational Mind*. Abingdon and New York: Routledge, 2020.

24 Ogden, Thomas H. *Conversations at the Frontier of Dreaming*. Northvale, NJ: Jason Aronson, 2001.

25 Hillman, J. *The Dream and the Underworld*. New York: Harper & Row, 1979, p. 96.

26 Hughes, Ted. *The Collected Poems of Ted Hughes*. London: Faber and Faber, 2005.

27 Wittgenstein, Ludwig. *Pensieri diversi [Philosophical Investigations]*. Italian translation. Milan: Adelphi, 1980.

28 Bion, Wilfred. *Cogitations*. London: Karnac Books, 1992, p. 38.

29 Bion, Wilfred. *Learning from Experience*. London: Karnac Books, 1984.

30 Bion, Wilfred. Bion, Wilfred Rupert. *A Memoir of the Future: The Past Presented*. London and New York: Routledge, 1990. The term "pictogram" was originally used by Piera Aulagnier to indicate a kind of pre-image that simultaneously contains a child's sensory area (for example, the mouth) and an object from the external world that engages with that area (in this case, the nipple).

31 Grotstein, James S. *Un raggio di intensa oscurità. L'eredità di Wilfred Bion [A Beam of Intense Darkness: Wilfred Bion's Legacy to Psychoanalysis]*. Italian translation. Milan: Raffaello Cortina, 2010.

32 Grotstein, James S. *Un raggio di intensa oscurità. L'eredità di Wilfred Bion [A Beam of Intense Darkness: Wilfred Bion's Legacy to Psychoanalysis]*. Italian translation. Milan: Raffaello Cortina, 2010.

33 Ferro, Antonino. *Tormenti di anime [Torments of the Soul]*. Milan: Raffaello Cortina, 2010.

34 Zambrano, María. *Il sogno creatore [The Creative Dream]*. Italian translation. Milan: Mondadori, 2002.
35 Lingiardi, V., and De Bei, F. "La terapia come processo di umanizzazione: Sogno e memoria nell'analisi di una paziente traumatizzata [Therapy as a humanizing process: Dream and memory in the analysis of a traumatized patient]." In *Trauma e psicopatologia [Trauma and Psychopathology]*, edited by V. Caretti and G. Craparo. Rome: Astrolabio, 2008, pp. 308–332.
36 Bromberg, Philip M. *Awakening the Dreamer: Clinical Journeys*. New York: Routledge, 2006, p. 20.
37 Bachelard, Gaston. *Psicoanalisi delle acque [Water and Dreams: An Essay on the Imagination of Matter]*. Italian translation. Como: Red, 1987.
38 Jung, Carl. *Analisi dei sogni [Dream Analysis]*. Italian translation. Turin: Boringhieri, 2003.

Chapter 9

This landscape is my father

Why is the spectacle of the sea so infinitely and eternally pleasing? Because the sea offers both the idea of immensity and the idea of movement. [...] Twelve or fourteen leagues of liquid in movement are enough to give the most lofty idea of beauty that has ever been offered to man in his transitory habitat.

Charles Baudelaire, *Intimate Journals: My Heart Laid Bare*[1]

What a beautiful dynamic object a path is!

Gaston Bachelard, *The Poetics of Space*[2]

Although we have all known mothers who are icy and fathers with a Mediterranean warmth, many people think of the mountains as a "paternal" place and the sea as a "maternal" place. One is vertical and masculine, the other is horizontal and feminine; one offers a spiritual ascent, the other offers a deep dive into amniotic fluids. But like all other binaries, this one is reductive and potentially risky, anchored as it is to stereotypes that make genders geographical and make postures moral. The danger of binarism is that it can create hierarchies, and we can drift into thinking that active is better than passive, spiritual is better than material, high is better than low. Value-laden translations of speech confirm this, since what is "superior," "elevated," and "supreme" is undoubtedly preferable to what is "inferior," "lowered," and "sunk." In her philosophical critique of rectitude, the Italian philosopher Adriana Cavarero[3] questions the moral and political meaning of the vertical position, and proposes that we rethink subjectivity in terms of *inclination*. In the classic figure of the *homo erectus* and in the rectifying devices of the

DOI: 10.4324/9781003252979-9

philosophical tradition, she sees self-referential ego lurking—closed and self-centered—while in the inclined figure she perceives an altruistic self taking shape, a self that is open and outstretched towards others. This reveals how any kind of extreme verticality hides a repression of dependence, of care and—at bottom—of childhood and motherhood.

Verticality and horizontality imprint concepts (hierarchies, genealogies, architectures, the direction of a gaze or a movement) that orient discourse and relationships. And they accompany us in the landscape. Winnicott dives enthusiastically into the idea that "the sea is the mother" and, in convincing us, he makes us forget that the Greeks' Poseidon and the Scandinavians' Ægir are sea creatures—lords of the Ocean. Sylvia Plath poignantly reminds us of this in a passage from her *Journals*:

> the association of the sea, which is a central metaphor for my childhood, my poems and the artist's subconscious, of the father image—relating to my own father, the buried male muse and god-creator risen to be my mate in Ted, to the sea-father Neptune—and the pearls and coral highly-wrought to art: pearls sea-changed from the ubiquitous grit of sorrow and dull routine.[4]

Aphrodite herself, who was born from the foam (*aphros*) of a wave—a froth formed when the emasculated Uranus's sperm was flung into the sea—is a victim of the high-low dichotomy, as we see in the Platonic concept of the two Aphrodites: the base one, for people who "love bodies more than their souls," and the higher one who (however) "does not participate in the nature of the female."[5] *Venus vulgaris* and *Venus coelestis* was what Marsilio Ficino called them, indicating that the latter, *Venus coelestis*, dwelled celestially in the supreme place of the universe, near the Cosmic Mind.

We have all seen the ways that the feminine gets split: the *sensual feminine* that sparks misogynist reaction from ascetics, and the *maternal feminine* that inspires and protects men. Jung hoped to mend this split symbolically (even while offering yet another verticalizing device): he gave great weight to the papal declaration on November 1, 1950, that Mary's body, as well as her soul, rose into heaven—that this was now a dogma of faith. This was "the most important religious event since the Reformation," according to the Swiss psychologist, "the only ray of light" in a Christianity that "has forgotten to develop its myth."

In this, the *Assumptio Mariae*, Jung saw the advent of a new anthropology, a change in the religious—and psychological—view of the relationship between spirit and matter: "Her human body, subject to the corruptibility of vile matter," is no longer only chthonic darkness, but is also celestial spirit.[6] If Mary was the Earth and God was Heaven, now Mary had become the Earth of Heaven.[7] And Earth in Heaven, too, for those who see her traditional blue cloak as the celestial vault that surrounds the Earth. The torment that Miguel de Unamuno projects in the landscape, the rose in the blue at the *summit* and the thorn in the greenery down in the *ravine*,[8] seems—for a moment—to subside into calm.

In every myth and in every religious tradition, ascensions and summits constitute a specific element of the spiritual experience: they include Mount Sinai (where Moses received the Ten Commandments), Mount Tabor (where Christ had his transfiguration), Mount Olympus, the Cosmic Mountain of the shamans, and Mount Kailash, a sacred mountain for Hindus, Buddhists, and Jains. Kailash, though, in its immense spiritual scope, dilutes its vertical thrust: tradition dictates that it should not be climbed, but that visitors should instead walk the 51 kilometers of its circumference. Its summit is shaped like a temple hosting Shiva and Parvati in an eternal embrace. The faithful believe that circling the whole base of Mount Kailash will free them from the sins of a lifetime and launch a new life. Not all mountains are made to be climbed; not all of them activate that vertical momentum, that virile performance. Even Freud—who breezily declared that woodpeckers, knives, and snakes were symbols for male genitalia, while shoes, rooms, and water springs were symbols for female genitals—attributed female sexual characteristics to a "landscape with a chapel, hill and wood" (in one dream analysis): he explained that—after all—the female pubis is also a mount, the *Mons Veneris*.[9]

Jung tells of a dreaming man who "stood on the slope of a mountain, under which lay a deep valley which contained a dark lake." The dreamer knew "that something had always held him back until then from approaching the lake," but this time "he decided to reach it." As he approached the shore, the atmosphere darkened and a sudden gust of wind rippled the surface of the water: "then, panic-stricken, he awoke." For Jung this was a dream that "shows the natural language of the symbol": the water is the depth of the unconscious, whose surface is agitated by an angel with "a healing power." (And there is a reference to the wind as a "breath that blows where it will.") The descent into the water, Jung says, is necessary, as is the disturbance by what we do not know, by what manifests itself spontaneously, without being invoked.[10]

In analyzing certain visions described by Miss Miller, Jung dwells on her image of a "bay of purple water." He traces the symbolism of the sea "to previous events" but does not shy away from etymological fascination with the word "bay" and its use to "designate something that remains open"; and he inevitably lands upon the characteristics of the female body and of maternity. He cites Faust and the reversal of mountain and sea that underpins the desire to reach the sun and "drink in its eternal light."[11] For Jung, the Faustian yearning marks every hero who feels the pull of the "mystery of rebirth and immortality" and thus the pull of a journey that leads him to the sea and downwards "into the jaws of death, that frighteningly narrow passage which heralds the new day."[12]

While Jungian dreams evoke heroes, deaths, and rebirths, the Freudian scenario leans toward genitals and sexuality. In Freud's writings on dreams there are many references to the landscape: no one before him— and perhaps no one since, except for Klein—had ever thought of sexualizing the non-human environment quite so broadly. And while "the complicated topography" of the female genitals shows why their representation in dreams leans on "*landscapes* with rocks, woods and water," "the imposing mechanism of the male sexual apparatus" is translated in dreams with all kinds of complicated and hard-to-describe "*machinery*."[13] In short, women get the complications of nature and men get the complications of mechanical things. Although it's also the case that, in the changing geography of the *Traumdeutung* (*The Interpretation of Dreams*) the mountain is a male symbol, which can become a female genital when garnished with "grass and bushes" and provided with "a forest" at the top.[14]

We have already mentioned landscape as a representation of the female genital. Mountain and rock are symbols of the male member; the garden, a frequent symbol of the female genital. The fruit does not stand for the child, but for the breast. Fierce animals mean sensually aroused people, and also evil impulses, passions. Blooms and flowers designate the woman's genital or, more specifically, virginity. Don't forget that flowers are really the genitalia of plants.[15]

This lost paradise of sexual symbols reminds me of a famous 1910 painting by Henri Rousseau that is coincidentally titled just that:

The Dream. A woman lying on a couch lost in a lush forest: is this a psychoanalytic couch?

Why on earth would an oneiric current link landscapes to genitalia? Because, Freud explains, this is how our unconscious recognizes the generative power of nature. And, he seems to imply, it invests the world with the psychic force of the sexual instinct. Further on the topic of dreams, genitals, and landscapes: Freud commented on experimentation done by a neurologist dear to him, Marcinowski, who would ask patients to draw their dream landscapes. To highlight the difference between the manifest meaning and the latent meaning of a dream, Freud explained that these drawings, "observed without malice," might look simply like panoramas or maps, but that "on closer inspection they reveal representations of the human body, of the genital organs," thus making possible "the understanding of the dream." The unconscious takes possession of the territory. Personality itself, said Freud in the *Introduction to Psychoanalysis*, can be represented as a geography, a territory that psychoanalysis must conquer by supporting the expansionist politics of the ego, draining the sea of the unconscious and transforming it into dry land, just as the Dutch did with the Zuiderzee.[16]

Freud loved walking in the mountains; he sent letters and postcards to his friends praising the beauty of the landscape there. In a famous dream of his own, a mountain guide carried him on his back "through changing landscapes." Moreover, on the subject of mountains, verticality, and horizontality, it is interesting to note that—for Freud—the "smooth walls on which one climbs [...] often with great anguish" represent "erect human bodies" that echo, in the dream, "the memory of the child's climbing up his parents and the people who assisted him." He adds that these "smooth" walls (verticals) are more likely to be men; when "laid tables and planks" (horizontals) are seen, they are more likely to be women.[17] Melanie Klein dwells on the experience of climbing. "Now I'm going to climb you: you are a mountain and I'm going to climb up,"[18] she notes about a child called Fritz. Her attention is focused on the geographies of the maternal body and how the child explores and names them. She explains this, for example, by illustrating the "imaginative game" in which Fritz slides a little dog onto his mother's body and imagines the path the dog traces: "The maternal breasts were mountains, and adjacent to the genital region there was a large river." Fritz, who around the age of five had shown a strong aversion to going out for walks, a total disinterest in getting familiar with his location, and no sense of direction at all, called all the extremities of his body "boundaries," and often repeated that "his mother was a mountain on which he climbed." A child called Richard, too, saw his mother as a mountain, and—according to Klein—the desire to climb her "symbolized the desire to have relations" with her. (Just as the fear of an approaching storm "immediately awakened the fear of being emasculated by the evil father.") This landscape orgy of Klein's also, of course, includes the sea (with ships, fish, shrimp, and starfish). Analyzing a dream-fantasy in which a child called John had been fighting "inside his mother's body, a struggle with the innumerable penises of the father (the shrimp)," Klein concludes that "in the general framework of the fantasy [...] both the sea and the house of flesh represented the mother's body." Anatomical, sexual, erotic: the parental landscape is a territory of urges, populated by desires and conflicts, for the two "parents" of psychoanalysis—Freud and Klein. But while Freud's concept of the unconscious seems to extend into the vastness of the external landscape, Klein's concept of the unconscious seems instead to incorporate the outside world (after having chopped it into bits).

Long gone are the days when psychoanalysis concretized its sexual theories in the landscape, treating dream images as "contents." For most psychoanalysts now (Bollas, for example, or Ferro), dreamscapes are cues for sharing and transforming emotions (or proto-emotions), for recognizing and naming affects, for narrating existences or making them narratable. The task of the analyst, as Bromberg would say,[19] is to help the patient build bridges between the islands of his dissociative states. To do so, one must *awaken the dreamer*, bring him into the session, and promote a dialogue between the dreaming patient and the wakeful patient. A dream is a "reality" to be experienced, rather than a mysterious object that needs deciphering.

We're still free, though, to dwell on some specific figures of landscape dreams—for example, verticality and horizontality. The psychoanalyst Stefano Bolognini suggests that this geometry can be traced back to infantile experiences that are sometimes destined to orient us to seek "environments consistent with these primitive fixations of ours"—to seek them in the external reality. Warning us against easy generalizations, Bolognini associates the horizontal dimension to an archaic type of functioning, not much differentiated from the maternal environment.

These dreams will often be "of a marine environment, a lacustrine and swimming environment," with a dreamer often "immersed in an idyllic nature" or a "stormy and hostile" nature, indicating the oscillation between the bliss of fusion and the struggle to survive a persecutory and ravenous maternal figure. "The absence of vertical figures," writes Bolognini, "protects the subject from any doubt about the fusional continuity between self and mother."[20]

The dynamics of the maternal and paternal *functions* contribute toward creating space, but the dialectic of bodies with spaces is more complex and less binary than we think. Mother is not *merely* the internal, secret, welcoming uterine environment, and father is not merely the external space, the launched, the ascendant, the phallic erection. There is not only the space of yes—the welcoming—and of no—the challenge and/or conquest. A walk in the mountains can be refreshing, embracing, and can offer a warm pause in a meadow. A swim in the open sea, or a sailboat race, can be a challenge, can be a trial, can be exhausting. And a balance between the forces at play can reconcile the vertical and horizontal harmonies of a landscape, as in a beautiful verse where Sandro Penna conjures the figure of a sailor who stretches his body to be nearly horizontal as he handles the vertical sail.[21] Or else it can tear them apart, in poetic perfection but in abysmal pain, as does Plath in her famous poem "I Am Vertical": over and over, she declares that she would prefer to be horizontal—that being horizontal suits her best, since she has neither the lifespan of a tree nor the splendid audacity of a flower. The poem ends with a stinging evocation of herself someday lying dead (and nourishing the plants with her corpse): maybe only then will she be touched by the trees; maybe only then will the flowers grant her a moment.[22]

In dreamwork, *landscapes* and *mindscapes* are valuable allies. The complexities of landscapes, their evidence and their hidden messages, their secrets and our own explorations, can help us understand cosmogonies that are anatomical, mental, and emotional—ours and other people's. And this is not only because—as Ferenczi says—it is not the sea that symbolizes the mother: the mother symbolizes the sea.[23] Also because, perhaps, a mountain is not always the symbol of a fearsome father. Sometimes it can "lower itself" to be a brother ("the Matterhorn is not only rock and ice, it's an older brother to me. [...] I need it, there are times when I feel the need to be close to it. It's a mystery how confident I can be with it").[24] It also happens that a person can reach for the peaks "because, down below, they just won't leave him alone."[25]

The landscape nuances to which we attribute parental functions or gender characteristics are infinite—with predictable recurrences and just as many denials. In the novel *The Eight Mountains*, Paolo Cognetti tells us a story of paternal silences and maternal teachings, of friendship and development, teaching us that, in the mountains "each one of us has a favorite altitude," "a landscape that resembles him and where he feels good." His mother's altitude "was undoubtedly the 1500-meter forest, the one of firs and larches, with blueberries, junipers, and rhododendrons growing in its shade, and deer hiding." He was "more attracted to the mountain that rises above that: alpine prairies, streams, peat bogs, high-altitude grasses, grazing animals." And then there was the place where "the vegetation disappears, the snow covers everything until early summer, and the prevailing color is the gray of the rock, veined by quartz and inlaid with the yellow of the lichens": there, his father's world began. And from his father he began "to learn how to go up into the mountains [...], the closest thing to an education I received from him."[26]

While Cognetti's Alps are paternal—at least from a certain height on up—it's the maternal Dolomite range that stands out in the Italian lyric poetry of the 20th century, in the verses of Antonia Pozzi: the Dolomites that embrace and bless, that occupy the evening like massive pregnant women.[27]

Rock is not only an erect pinnacle; water is not only moisture from springs. Let's avoid burdening geography with the gender binarism that has—for too long—marked and simplified psychoanalysis. I'd like to use a "false memory" to illustrate the complexity of our gender identifications with our parents. (And I'll also reveal one of the autobiographical impulses for writing this book.) For many years, I thought of my father as a mountain man and thought of my mother as a woman of the sea. On the basis of this idea, I also developed many fantasies about the maternal and the paternal. But when I worked more carefully on my memories, and freed them from coverings of various kinds, fresh recollections emerged: I recalled a father with whom I used to go swimming and take long excursions at the seaside (while my mother would anxiously admonish us to not swim until three hours after eating), and of a mother who held my hand along alpine footpaths. The person who taught me to delight in the sea's embrace, in the joy of diving and snorkeling, is my father. When I see mountain peaks on the horizon, the melancholy voice I hear is from my mother, agonizing over the unthinkability of infinity. My pleasure in the sea, therefore, is a paternal gift; and soaring feelings, imbued with spirituality, are my maternal inheritance. As Stephen Mitchell[28] recounted in a personal reconstruction of his own, it is likely that our evolutionary paths are littered with "gender traps" that sometimes make us deposit memories and identifications in spots that seem most appropriate or desirable. Perhaps I—in desiring a more watery mother and a more spiritual father—ended up repositioning them in the geography of my desires.

But are there the peaks without valleys? Are there bold descents without ascents? Can we have Mount Kailash and Olympus without Keats and his "vale of Soul-making"? Psychoanalysis has finally surrendered to the idea that our identifications with parental figures are multiple, intertwined, and not simply one identification as the opposite of the other, as Jessica Benjamin would say.[29] Consequently, the construction of our gender identities is always inclusive: all ways of being in relationship with the other are necessary.

The search for the father may turn out to be a geological genealogy.[30]

The themes of classical psychoanalysis—particularly Oedipal vicissitudes—now come up against more articulated concepts, with stories that are more personal and less universal. The sunny trivium of Oedipal patricide ("O trivium! O secret valley! O forest! O gorge where three roads meet!"[31]), and the steep walls that loom over the encounter with the Sphinx can become new landscapes where the encounter with knowledge can take place in ways that are more *inclined*, more accessible, more generative. In the iconography of Oedipus facing the Sphinx—in works by Ingres, de Chirico, and Bacon, for example—one clearly sees in the background the threat of the gaping and horrific vaginas, ready to swallow anyone who cannot solve the riddle.

While Schnitzler, in his witty writing on psychoanalysis, complains about the Oedipus complex being over-valued, Ferro (in his book of "irreverent thoughts") denounces the glare of the Oedipus myth that—like the glaring light pollution from streetlights that washes out the stars in the night sky—has prevented us from seeing and studying other constellations and other myths.[32] On the basis of clinical experience and hundreds of studies in the field of parenting, for example, we can now confirm that maternal and paternal functions can be performed independently of biological sex. We need to study and metabolize new relational configurations and, to do so, we must renounce the excesses of Oedipal literalism.

Moving from the Oedipus complex to Oedipal complexity, we will be able to consider new paternal geometries, perhaps with the help of new landscapes and the capacity to sit in the uncertainty that Keats claims for poetry and Stevens evokes in his verses on "The Irish Cliffs of Moher"—where he asks who is his father and then concludes that perhaps the landscape itself is his father: earth and sea and air.[33]

An element is never just that one element. The bipolarity of Jungian psychology (which owes a debt to the *I Ching*) teaches us not to trust univocal polarizations and helps us to seek, even to imagine, the high in the low, the feminine in the masculine, the white in the black, the sea in the mountain, the liquid in the solid. Horace-Bénédict de Saussure, the founder of alpinism, perceived liquid in a solid when he was able to perceive, in the Glacier des Bois atop Mont Blanc, a "sea that suddenly froze, not in a stormy moment, but in the instant in which the wind has calmed down and the waves, though very high, are blunted and rounded."[34] Or when, looking at Mont Blanc, he had the geological vision, the intuition that allowed him to grasp the sea in the structure of the Alpine massif.[35]

I think about the region of Liguria, where green hillsides plunge into the sea, and I discover that its traditional music has songs such as: "Over this mountain / the sailor sails; / without a boat, he climbs / high above the path of the sea," or "Calm sea of mountains, and sea of fields / high mountains of water, here in front." We are not obliged to stitch opposites together; often we must just accept them as such. Rejecting a forced binarism does not mean we must promote a gray equidistance in order to eliminate contrast; it just means we must bring those elements close together, sustaining their tension and uncertainty; sustaining the disjunction and the encounter that are at the base of psychic dialogue and synthesis. Each of us seeks a distant landscape (sometimes without realizing that we are seeking it). At times, after having resisted it at length, we abandon ourselves to it. At times, once we've reached the summit, we discover—like the great English mountaineer Edward Whymper—that "higher up there is nothing to see; everything is down below."

After all, can we possibly think only of "regression" in relation to the sea—when Nietzsche invites us to navigate on the sea because it sets our thoughts sailing? The ocean of becoming? "Away on the ships, philosophers!"[36] Can mountains possibly spark only ideas like "challenge" and "freezing" and "asceticism," when mountains also mean earth and forest, meditation and discovery? The discovery, Meltzer would say, is the discovery of thoughts waiting to be discovered: that vibrate in the waiting, in the darkness like a "deer, which grazes at night, noticed by its darting white tail." Those are the tiny movements of the object that we catch sight of while they take their first steps toward creating meaning, "receptive imagination, open to the possible, unconcerned with probability."[37] I can't help recalling María Zambrano's "forest glades" (and not only because of the natural setting). Places "where it is not always possible to enter," places observed by standing on the threshold, where "the appearance of a few animal footprints" is not enough to "take the step." *Mindscapes* where the oxymoron flashes bright and the logos is "submerged" and is an expression of pathos. I can't help seeing Meltzer's deer and then Zambrano's deer, "this groove just opened in the air, this trembling of leaves, [...] the shadow of the fleeing animal, a deer who is perhaps wounded too, the wound that remains in the forest glade."[38] And I can't help seeing the English poet Ted Hughes's "thought-fox"— which is both the animal that flees and the poetic verse that stops it (in his poem "The Thought Fox").

I imagine this midnight moment's forest:
Something else is alive
Beside the clock's loneliness
And this blank page where my fingers move.

Through the window I see no star:
Something more near
Though deeper within darkness
Is entering the loneliness:

Cold, delicately as the dark snow
A fox's nose touches twig, leaf;
Two eyes serve a movement, that now
And again now, and now, and now

Sets neat prints into the snow
Between trees, and warily a lame

Shadow lags by stump and in hollow
Of a body that is bold to come

Across clearings, an eye,
A widening deepening greenness,
Brilliantly, concentratedly,
Coming about its own business

Till, with a sudden sharp hot stink of fox
It enters the dark hole of the head.
The window is starless still; the clock ticks,
The page is printed.[39]

A 1967 photograph by Richard Long, titled *A Line Made by Walking*, marks a fundamental moment in contemporary art (it has been compared to Malevich's *Black Square*): it announces, in a critical way with respect to the territorial intrusiveness of American land art, the advent of the artist's body in the landscape. It shows a meadow at the edge of a forest and the trace of a path created by the photographer repeatedly going back and forth.

This trampled grass intentionally immortalizes the presence/absence of the artist, while many other paths—urban and not—have a character that is involuntary, unforeseen, and irregular in the manner of the "Third landscapes" intuited by Gilles Clément (and which we'll touch on later). These paths are "unplanned," wrote the Lacanian psychoanalyst Massimo Recalcati; they are generated by the marginal walking of passers-by; these are paths that "cut through our canonical trajectories, appear as if in a dream, and seem to begin and end in nothingness."[40]

Heidegger spoke of *Holzwege*, forest paths that are often overgrown and that break off abruptly. Simon Schama was harsh about this in his *tour de force*, the book *Landscape and Memory*.[41] Schama is irritated by the lucubration of continental philosophy and outraged by Heidegger's Nazi aura, which extends to an entire "Germanic typology" of relationships with nature marked by mythical and magical origins, and which includes Jung and Nietzsche and reaches up to the present-day landscape artworks of Anselm Kiefer. Schama's irritation in the face of these mythological/landscape irrationalities—with their hint of Wagner—is understandable, but we cannot ignore the visual power and the psychic valence of "trails in the woods." We have all walked such paths, discovering that "each goes its separate way, though within the same forest. It often appears as if one is identical to another. But it only appears so. Woodcutters and forest keepers know these paths."[42]

The woodland patrimony that populates our *mindscapes* is endless: from Dante's "dark forest" to the woods of Ariosto's *Orlando Furioso* ("they came to where the path was lost in the forest"), from Grimm's fairy tales to the arboreal world of Calvino's *Baron in the Trees*, from the poet Zanzotto's *Galateo in bosco* to the multiple versions of the forest in "Rashomon." These different paths—often intertwined in problematic ways (as Zambrano's is intertwined with Heidegger)—lead us to value the unsaturated and *chiaroscuro* aspects of the forest. I wanted to explore the intermittent traces of some trails here (with all the pleasure that comes from losing the main path sometimes)... to explore those intangible glades that, Zambrano would say, make the world habitable.

Notes

1 Baudelaire, Charles. *Mon coeur mis à nu: journal intime [Intimate Journals: My Heart Laid Bare]*, 1887.
2 Excerpt from *The Poetics of Space* by Gaston Bachelard. Translated by Maria Jolas, copyright © 1958 by Presses Universitaires de France. Translation copyright © 1964 by Penguin Random House LLC. Used by permission of Penguin Classics, an imprint of Penguin Publishing Group, a division of Penguin Random House LLC. All rights reserved.
3 Cavarero, Adriana. *Inclinazioni. Critica della rettitudine [Inclinations. A Critique of Rectitude]*. Milan: Raffello Cortina, 2014.
4 Plath, Sylvia. *The Journals of Sylvia Plath, 1950–1962*, edited by Karen V. Kukil. London: Faber and Faber, 2000.
5 Plato, *Symposium*, c. 385–370 BC.
6 Jung, Carl. *Risposta a Giobbe [Answer to Job]*. Italian translation in *Opere*, Vol. 11. Turin: Boringhieri, 1979.
7 Bianchi, E. "Maria, Terra del Cielo [Mary, Land of Heaven]," in *Maria. Testi teologici e spirituali dal I al XX secolo [Mary. Theological and Spiritual Texts from the 1st to the 20th Centuries]*, edited by the Comunità di Bose. Milan: Mondadori, 2000, pp. ix–lxxiii.
8 De Unamuno, M. *Nostra Signora di Marzo (Canzoniere 941) [Our Lady of March (Songbook 941)]*. Italian translation in *Maria. Testi teologici e spirituali dal I al XX secolo [Mary. Theological and Spiritual Texts from the 1st to the 20th Centuries]*, edited by the Comunità di Bose. Milan: Mondadori, 2000, p. 1349.

9 Freud, Sigmund. "Symbolism in Dreams," in *The Standard Edition of the Complete Psychological Works*, Vols. 1–24. London: The Hogarth Press and the Institute of Psychoanalysis, 1953–1974.

10 Jung, Carl. *Gli archetipi dell'inconscio collettivo [The Archetypes and The Collective Unconscious]*. Italian translation in *Opere*, Vol. 9, book 1. Turin: Boringhieri, 1980.

11 Goethe, Johann Wolfgang von. *Faust*, 1831.

12 Jung, Carl. *Simboli della trasformazione [Symbols of Transformation]*. Italian translation in *Opere*, Vol. 5. Turin: Boringhieri, 1970.

13 Freud, Sigmund. "Symbolism in Dreams," in *The Standard Edition of the Complete Psychological Works*, Vols. 1–24. London: The Hogarth Press and the Institute of Psychoanalysis, 1953–1974.

14 Freud, Sigmund. *The Interpretation of Dreams*, in *The Standard Edition of the Complete Psychological Works*, Vols. 1–24. London: The Hogarth Press and the Institute of Psychoanalysis, 1953–1974.

15 Freud, Sigmund. *New Introductory Lectures on Psycho-Analysis and Other Works*, in *The Standard Edition of the Complete Psychological Works*, Vols. 1–24. London: The Hogarth Press and the Institute of Psychoanalysis, 1953–1974.

16 Freud, Sigmund. *New Introductory Lectures on Psycho-Analysis and Other Works*, in *The Standard Edition of the Complete Psychological Works*, Vols. 1–24. London: The Hogarth Press and the Institute of Psychoanalysis, 1953–1974.Interestingly, Lacan (*Il Seminario. Libro xxii [The Seminar. Book XXII]*. Italian translation, Rome: Astrolabio, 2005) re-reads Freud's famous line, "where It was, shall I be" in a different way, a way that is not "disciplinary" (Recalcati, Massimo, *Il mistero delle cose. Nove ritratti d'artista [The Mystery of Things. Nine Artist's Portraits]*. Milan: Feltrinelli, 2016); Lacan "pushes" toward subjectivizing it. In this case, it's not that the Ego must "dislodge" the Id and take its place, but rather that the Ego that must go to where the unconscious sits, where the subject's desire is originally inscribed, in its constitutive otherness… and that—in that location—it must "happen," it must be revealed. So, in other words: "Where It was, I (je) shall happen": I must happen in the place of the unconscious.

17 Freud, Sigmund. *The Interpretation of Dreams*, in *The Standard Edition of the Complete Psychological Works*, Vols. 1–24. London: The Hogarth Press and the Institute of Psychoanalysis, 1953–1974.

18 Klein, Melanie. The quoted excerpts are from these Italian translations of her work (in *Scritti [Writings]*. Turin: Boringhieri, 1978: "Lo sviluppo di un bambino [The Development of a Child]" (1921, pp. 17–73), "Il complesso edipico alla luce delle angosce primitive [The Oedipal Complex in the Light of Primitive Anxieties]" (1945, pp. 355–408), and "Contributo alla teoria dell'inibizione intellettiva [Contribution to the theory of intellectual inhibition]" (1931, pp. 269–281). The child, "Fritz," was none other than Erich, the youngest of the three children of Klein herself.

19 Bromberg, Philip M. *Awakening the Dreamer: Clinical Journeys*. New York: Routledge, 2006, p. 20.

20 Bolognini, Stefano. *Lo zen e l'arte di non sapere cosa dire [Zen and the Art of Not Knowing What to Say]*. Turin: Boringhieri, 2010.

21 Penna, Sandro. *Sul molo il vento soffia forte [On the Pier, a Strong Wind Blows]*. In *Poesie, prose e diari [Poetry, Prose, and Diaries]*. Milan: Mondadori, 2017.

22 Plath, Sylvia. *Collected Poems*. London: Faber and Faber, 2002.

23 Ferenczi, Sándor. *Thalassa. Saggio sulla teoria della genitalità [Thalassa: A Theory of Genitality]*. Italian translation. Milan: Raffaello Cortina, 1993.

24 Barmasse, Hervé; interview with Paolo Cognetti: "Cento volte sulla vetta, il Cervino è mio fratello [One hundred times on the summit, the Matterhorn is my brother]" in *La Repubblica—Robinson*, March 26, 2017, pp. 10–11.

25 Cognetti, Paolo. *Le otto montagne [The Eight Mountains]*. Turin: Einaudi, 2018.

26 Cognetti, Paolo. *Le otto montagne [The Eight Mountains]*. Turin: Einaudi, 2018.

27 Pozzi, Antonia. "Le madri montagne [The mother mountains]," in *Poesie 1933–1938 [Poems 1933–1938]*. Milan: Garzanti, 2001.

28 Mitchell, Stephen A. "Gender and sexual orientation in the age of post-modernism: The plight of the perplexed clinician." *Gender and Psychoanalysis* 1 (1996), pp. 45-73.

29 Benjamin, Jessica. *Like Subjects, Love Objects: Essays on Recognition and Sexual Difference*. New Haven: Yale University Press, 1995.

30 Magrelli, Valerio. *Geologia di un padre [Geology of a Father]*. Turin: Einaudi, 2013.

31 Sophocles. *Oedipus Rex*, c. 429 BC.

32 Ferro, Antonino. "Omogenitorialità: Un pensiero in cerca di pensatore [Homoparenting: A thought in search of a thinker]," *Giornale Italiano di Psicologia* 43, no. 1–2 (2016), pp. 133–136. Ferro, A., *Pensieri di uno psicoanalista irriverente [Thoughts of an Irreverent Psychoanalyst]*. Milan: Raffaello Cortina, 2017.

33 Stevens, Wallace. *The Collected Poems*. London: Faber and Faber, 2006.

34 De Saussure, Horace Bénédict. *La scoperta del Monte Bianco [The Discovery of Mont Blanc]*, in "Voyages dans les Alpes [Voyages in the Alps]." Italian translation. Turin: Vivalda, 2012. See also Meschiari, M. *Terra Sapiens. Antropologie del paesaggio [Terra Sapiens. Anthropologies of the Landscape]*. Palermo: Sellerio, 2010.

35 De Saussure: "I saw the sea that once covered the entire surface of the globe, forming, through deposits and successive crystallizations, first the primitive mountains and then the secondary ones [...]. I then saw the waters rushing into open and emptied chasms by the explosion of elastic fluids, and [...] carry over great distances the huge blocks that we find scattered across our plains. Finally, I saw, after the retreat of the waters, the seedlings of plants and animals, fertilized by the newly produced air, begin to develop,

both on the land abandoned by the waters and in the very water that had pooled in the surface cavities" (pp. 136–137).

36 Nietzsche, Friedrich. *Aurora*. Italian translation. Milan: Adelphi, 1978; and Nietzsche, *La gaia scienza e Idilli di Messina [The Joyful Wisdom and Idylls from Messina]*. Italian translation. Milan: Adelphi, 1977.

37 Meltzer, Donald. *Creativity and the countertransference*. In *The Vale of Soulmaking*, edited by M. H. Williams. London: Karnac, 2005, pp. 175–182, p. 182.

38 Zambrano, María. *Chiari del bosco [Forest Glades]*. Italian translation. Milan: Feltrinelli, 1991.

39 Hughes, Ted. "The Thought Fox," in *The Collected Poems of Ted Hughes*. London: Faber and Faber, 2005.

40 Recalcati, Massimo. "I sentieri invisibili che nascono nelle nostre città [The invisible paths that spring up in our cities]" remarks on the photography of Antonio Costa. *La Repubblica—Robinson*, April 10, 2017.

41 Schama, Simon. *Landscape and Memory*. New York: Knopf, 1995.

42 Heidegger, Martin. *Off the Beaten Track*, edited and translated by Julian Young and Kenneth Haynes. New York: Cambridge University Press, 2002.

Chapter 10

Reverberation

If the pages of this book offer some felicitous line or other, may the reader pardon me the discourtesy of having claimed it first.

Jorge Luis Borges, *Fervor of Buenos Aires*[1]

And doesn't the rock become a full-fledged you, the moment I speak to it?

Novalis, *The Disciples at Saïs*[2]

In our stroll through psychoanalysis and landscape, we can lean on an elegant sort of "walking stick": the concept of *retentissement*. This concept—which was very dear to Minkowski, and which was later developed by Bachelard, and then was rediscovered by Bollas—helps us to describe the essence of a poetic image and its evocative power.[3] We could translate it as an "echo," or even better as a "reverberation," to indicate that phenomenon when a reader is so captivated by some verses that he feels as if he himself was the poet. Indeed, he feels that that imagery—that poem—is for him, is *his*. While resonance is a thing that scatters across the various planes of our existence, reverberation carries us into the depths. With resonance we hear the poem; with reverberation we speak it. The poet and the reader react in the same way to the imagery: they are captured in their identity/identicalness. Moreover, the experience of *retentissement* sparks a poetic intensity in the reader that emerges spontaneously, pre-psychologically. Affective resonances and memories come later. The very understanding of poetry comes *later*. It's as if the verses come from a place inside the poet and reach a place inside the reader, without stirring their surfaces at all. It's as if image,

DOI: 10.4324/9781003252979-10

psyche, and language seek each other out until they coincide, in a perfect neural meter of poetic beats.[4] That's what happens to me when I read the first tercet of this poem by Sandro Penna:

Night and sweet wind: hide me—
cast out from my home, I came to you,
my romantic ancient slow river.[5]

The opening echoes Leopardi (Leopardi's line "Sweet and clear is the night and without wind" becomes Penna's "Night and sweet wind: hide me"),[6] but also echoes Dante ("The night that hides things from us"), and it prepares me for the fluvial consolation of the wonderful hendecasyllable *"mio romantico antico fiume lento"*[7] and for the peace of its internal repetition, in *"romantico/antico."* In the reverberation, the triplet of Penna delivers me simultaneously to the poetry and to the landscape: it promotes a *poetic action*; it inaugurates a form.

James Hillman argues that the mind has a "poetic basis." This formula has taken hold in the Jungian field, but mainly—I fear—because it is tautologically understood as *poetic*. Few readers dwell on its existential implications—that is, on the (neo-Platonic) centrality of imagination and aesthetics to our psychological lives. Do not think—Hillman seems to say—that images count less than facts in your lives.

I do not agree with the unnecessarily polemical way that he contrasts the poetic mind with the physiology of the brain.[8] Rather, it appears that the poetic form—brevity, rhythm, rhyme, immediacy of images, intersubjective comprehension, and so on—activates our neurons in specific and complex ways. A tenacious passion for neuroscience prompted the English writer A. S. Byatt to comment on two famous lines by John Donne: "License my roving hands, and let them go, / Before, behind, between, above, below."[9]

I think—though this cannot be proved, and for that reason is merely a hypothetical folly—that Donne's adverbs of a flow of movement, like his enumeration of parts of an imagined face, are an appeal to mirror neurones. And the mirror neurones that respond to "Before, behind, between, above, below" are not picture-making neurones, but locations on the body of both writer and reader. They are the more powerful because they are purely brief firings in the mind of its deep habit of imagining motion in the body, and linking these images to other emotions, to form concepts and map them with grammar.[10]

The neuroscientists and psychologists who study the relationship between brain and language consider poetry to be one of the brain events that contributes to "building" the reality in which we live.[11] *Paterson*, a Jim Jarmusch movie, exemplifies this impeccably by recounting the poetry of things that cannot be seen: days repeating over and over; the movement of objects that do not move; vague disquiet and the company of short poems spoken as they arise, within the mind-world of the poet, who—in this case—is a bus driver. The poetry is just short lines; the poems use rhyming and formal figures that allow for a reading of the world that is immediate, deep, rhythmic. An experience that I described like this: "Swimming is like reading / Immersed in a hum / of sound cadences in the head. / Pages, laps. / The nautical perfection / that strengthens the soul."[12]

The way that reverberating experience participates in the construction of reality includes the simultaneous attempt to endow it with meaning and to find/create—in ourselves and in the external world—a home for our emotional experiences. "The Poets light but Lamps."[13]

Bollas's parents were "very much in love before the war," but when his father returned home, a strange distance and "a mood of sad vexation pervaded the house." The future psychoanalyst, just a child at the time, grew melancholy from this change of climate. At school, he tells us, he unconsciously chose an object, a swing, "to conserve some aspects of this self state." He could not explain why, but he imagined that the swing, which amused him so much and which he felt was so suited as "an object for a joyful two-person relation," could—when empty and abandoned—signify "the absence of such pleasure."[14] Even now, he concludes, when he happens to see a swing in a playground, he relives something of that emotional experience.

Like a line of poetry, a place or an object can reverberate in us, giving (and giving-back) a personal meaning built from distant sensory and emotional experiences. Because they continue to maintain their intrinsic value, we can say that they occupy an intermediate area between their conventional use and our personal understanding. We could even suggest that, just as the *affordance*[15] of a fruit is in the service of our survival (its form appeals to us, and experience tells us whether it's nutritious or poisonous) and of our physical development—even in an evolution-ary sense—likewise the choice of certain objects arises from their ability be at the service of the aesthetical survival of our psychic life.

In an encounter with the object, Bollas would say, we feel "the hand of fate,"[16] a sort of initiation that disturbs and grabs us, a search in the future for something that dwells in memory. "When we use an object, it is as if we know the terms of the engagement."[17] We know that we are entering an intermediate space, where the nature of perception changes and our subjectivity is liberated. Our relationship with the object will have changed forever—changed both the object and ourselves as well. This is true for a swing in a rundown playground, and for a song, for a musical phrase, for a particular landscape.

Charles Simic compares his poems to a table on which he arranges items he picked up while walking: a stone, a feather, a nail. They sit there for months; he looks at them and thinks about them until he sees associations among them.[18]

Our psychic life develops in an intermediate area inhabited by the balances and tensions between our objects and the objects of the world. It's a gravitational field in which the outside enters our imagination, which in turn penetrates the landscape. For the Irish poet Seamus Heaney, this intermediate world is where nature meets the names and legends of a place, and they all come to life, making us inhabitants not only of a geographical country but also of a "country of the mind." It is "the sense of place," the link between a landscape and a poet, and the poet knows and loves the landscape in two opposite and complemen-tary ways: the "lived illiterate and unconscious" way and the "learned, literate and conscious" way.[19] Poetry is born from this tension.

Recalling Wordsworth, the poet of lakes in the landscape, Bollas[20] speaks of a poetic investiture of the world that draws nourishment from childhood, when the child, with his imagination, makes the earth roil with his feelings, as if it were the sea.[21] It is here that our relationship with the landscape begins, in the space suspended amid fantasy, place, and memory.

Just a few lines are all we need—just the image of a woman looking out of her window—to show that the landscape is always inside and outside, is always a contemporaneous discovery of oneself and of the world: "The Angle of a Landscape—That every time I wake." The window belongs to Emily Dickinson's lonely room, where the branch of a pine tree can turn

into a sea ("By my Window have I for Scenery / Just a Sea—with a Stem")
and "It—suggests to our Faith / They—suggest to our Sight."[22]

Psychoanalysts love Robert Frost (Ogden and Bromberg give him a
place of honor in their writings) and perhaps that's because for Frost a
poem is an *arrest of disorder*. A poem is an affirmation, the truth of
which is balanced between the two meanings of *disorder*: confusion and
disease. "Each poem," says Frost, "clarifies something."

> But then you've got to do it again. You can't get clarified to stay so:
> let you not think that. In a way, it's like nothing more than blowing
> smoke rings. Making little poems encourages a man to see that there
> is a shapeliness in the world. A poem is an arrest of disorder.[23]

As so often happens, it is or yearns to be a therapeutic session.

When Bromberg was asked what aspects of his personal history had
most influenced his interest in psychoanalysis, he replied: "I think the
most important factor was the relationship with my mother. Not only did
she write poetry, but she was a poet by nature." For Bromberg, poetry
helps to capture that part of the analytical relationship that is "lost in
translation." And where does this famous expression, *lost in translation*,
come from? Apparently it comes from Frost himself, who allegedly uttered
these words during an interview: "Poetry is what is lost in translation."
And right after that, he said: "It is also what is lost in interpretation."[24]

Ogden considered poetry to be a great exercise in analytical listening.[25] So much so that he chose a poem, Frost's "Acquainted with the
Night," and compared it to a session with his patient. Writing a poem,
and reading a poem, are actions that entail a strong ability to choose
and to purify one's language. It is *the music of what happens* (a phrase
that Ogden borrowed from Seamus Heaney for the title of his paper):
the rhythm of the session, of the relationship. Perhaps, Ogden says, "we
turn to poetry and psychoanalysis in part with the hope that we might
reclaim (or experience for the first time) forms of human aliveness that
we have foreclosed to ourselves."[26]

Ogden writes about poetry for the pure pleasure of it; he is not concerned with its utility. His readers can use his chapters as they wish, finding (or not finding) connections between a poem and the way a session
unfolds. His writing, he reiterates, can like a poem be as useful or as futile
as a stroll. "Walks are useless," says the American poet Archie Ammons,

"So are poems [...] a walk doesn't mean anything, which is a way of say-ing that to some extent it means anything you can make it mean—and always more than you can make it mean."[27] *A poem is a walk*. Here again we see the paths and *the line made by walking*.

The poetic word is a chosen word—chosen more or less uncon-sciously. It is an attempt, perhaps the final attempt, to bestow meaning on things, to recompose them by means of a creative discipline (which only seems to be an oxymoron). It is the place where, at that point and in that moment, you can feel better—where disorder stops. But it is a word that is familiar with the invasion of desire or the pain of loss. Leopardi's inspiration was always melancholy; Wallace Stevens consid-ered poetry to be "a violence from within that protects us from a vio-lence without [...] The imagination pressing back against the pressure of reality."[28]

Lacan showed us the distance between reality and that which is real.[29] Beautiful or ugly, *reality* is what is. In its ordinary flow there is repetition, there is a "reassuring" return of the same things: objects that we trust for their stability. The *real* is what upends this picture, something that goes overboard and wakes us up "from the sleep of reality": the diagnosis of an illness, the end of a relationship, a falling in love that overwhelms our usual habits, a nightmare. The real, we could say, barges into reality. Compared to the sleep of reality, we could say that poetry is the wakeful-ness of what's real. In a kinship with the experience of dreaming (even daydreaming), the poetic function can be an attempt—not always a suc-cessful attempt—to restore a trusting relationship with reality, without which we would become psychotic. Even a poet, Baudelaire would say, moves through a "forest of symbols,"[30] but—unlike a psychotic—a poet can decide to get out of it. When the real barges into reality, "reality is so heavy that the hand gets tired, and no form can contain it. Memory then runs to the most fantastical enterprises (spaces, verses, rhymes, times)."[31] These fantastical enterprises produce verses and rhymes; these are aes-thetic solutions for facing the real while also circumscribing its incandes-cence. A poem is an arrest of disorder because, while reconstructing order, it protects the *midworld* from the traumatic incursions that inter-rupt the continuity of psychic life. *The Redress of Poetry*, Heaney called it, as the title to his collected essays on poetry.[32]

I wrote my first poem in the early 1980s, in a waiting room of the national cancer institute in Milan, where my mother was a patient.

Without knowing why, I picked up a piece of paper and wrote a few lines. Then I realized that it was a way to give a shape to my pain, to contain it, and also to look at the pain through a special language, a language that was new to me but also familiar. Poetry can become a way of observing the world and moving through the world. A line arrives; you welcome it; you spend some time taking it apart and putting it back together again and—if you are able or lucky—you find the exact point where image meets language. That's when poetry can be a rescue, *a momentary stay against confusion.*[33] A movement of the mind that resists the intrusion of the outside world and re-establishes a temporary but redeeming sense of cohesion and continuity. This is where the landscape becomes a founding element of this movement, a psychic object embedded in the verses. Verses and landscape are indistinguishable—inside and outside—like a Möbius strip, like a poem by Heaney or Penna.

A poem is not only a way of getting in touch with objects and landscape; it's also a way to evoke place and time while shut in a room. That's the movement that Ted Hughes tried to capture in his *Birthday Letters*, where the poetry is an attempt "to open a direct, private, inner contact with [Sylvia ...] to evoke her presence to myself, and to feel her there listening."[34] Poetry digs for memories that inhabited our disorder—it digs for objects we had lost.

> Remember how we picked the daffodils?
> Nobody else remembers, but I remember.
> [...] But somewhere your scissors remember. Wherever they are.
> Here somewhere, blades wide open,
> April by April
> Sinking deeper
> Through the sod—an anchor, a cross of rust.[35]

It fuses a type of experience that is neither reality nor fantasy, but an intermediate realm that I would call the "poetic real." Important things happen there.

Writing poetry keeps us in the world while it saves us from the world. *A poem is the actualized love of desire that remains a desire.*[36]

In his composition "The Most of It," Frost speaks of a man who launches a love call across a lake and gets back an echo. The man keeps looking at the lake, and then a deer appears.

As a great buck it powerfully appeared,
Pushing the crumpled water up ahead,
And landed pouring like a waterfall,
And stumbled through the rocks with horny tread,
And forced the underbrush—and that was all.[37]

What was that *all?* Just a deer, Ogden says, but also the unexpected appearance of that last verse: *and that was all.* A new voice, an unexpected voice. As unexpected as the deer, which thus becomes "a poetic creature." "Creatures of silence came out of the forest glades, from dens and bushes," wrote Rilke.[38] Here we see Meltzer's thoughts waiting to be discovered, which vibrate in the darkness like a deer, grazing at night, seen by its white tail darting off. Here we see Zambrano's wounded deer, announced in the forest glade by the trembling leaves. Here is Stevens's pheasant, "disappearing in the brush."[39]

Pictograms as the visual basis of thought: unconscious (often imperceptible) images that give rise to conscious narratives. This is how Sylvia Plath describes the birth of a poem and the transformation (perhaps a Bionian transformation?) that it carries:

A door opens, a door shuts. In between you have had a glimpse: a garden, a person, a rainstorm, a dragonfly, a heart, a city… I think of those round glass Victorian paperweights… a clear globe, self-complete, very pure, with a forest or village or family group within it. You turn it upside down, then back. It snows. Everything is changed in a minute. It will never be the same in there—not the fir trees, nor the gables, nor the faces. So a poem takes place.[40]

For the poet, thinking and writing are not disjointed, sequential actions. The link between thinking and writing can be reversed, so that sometimes instead of writing what we think, we find ourselves thinking what we write. As if we give birth to what we think without knowing it. Then we write it down, to find it, there, in the verses.

Writing thus becomes a way of thinking, with ideas that come out of our fingers like sensory intuitions that we feel are ours, without us knowing how they will develop and where they will take us. Even in the most difficult moments, we are not alone; we are with the other person who reads our words, and with the other person whose words we have read;

the point of view of those who have gone before us and who we recreate by reading them. It is a process of growth, Ogden says, which we apply to our own parents and to our analysts; killing them metaphorically is as necessary as commemorating them. To commemorate them we perform a *metamorphical* internalization, because at the moment we transform them into aspects of ourselves (as in an identification), what we assimilate is a version of them that we have already transformed in order to be able to use it fully.[41] We carry within us not just our significant people, but also poems, paintings, music, and landscapes. They group together as interior families, genealogies.

What did I *understand* about what I *wrote* by reverberations and disseminations? I'll try to trace a path. I think that poetic verse and landscape mirror one another, mediated by our possibility of reverberating both of them, of feeling them to be our own. The reverberating experience occurs in a relationship between two objects: the poet's voice immerses itself in our imaginal depths, and this encounter creates a transformation. The *poetic investiture* coming from the world creates a *midworld* whose reality is not purely subjective nor purely objective: it is poetic. We could call it the "cycle of *retentissement*": real objects (a poem, a landscape) meet psychic objects, and become evocative objects (a poem, a landscape). The place of this encounter is never safe: it must be guarded and protected from the inevitable and necessary irruptions of reality. The poetic verses can limit the invasion, like a filter; can attempt to remediate when the pain or confusion are too powerful. For this reason, the verses are also a window: "a sample of a freedom compromised / by the presence of fate; / which among us equals / the great excess of the outside world."[42]

A poem is disorienting because it continually transitions among poet, landscape, and reader. It has its own passport, as Bromberg would say, for traveling across the states of the self that are suspended between spaces.[43]

In a field
I am the absence
of field.
This is
always the case.
Wherever I am
I am what is missing.

When I walk
I part the air
and always
the air moves in
to fill the spaces
where my body's been.

We all have reasons
for moving.

I move
to keep things whole.[44]

Once again, it is a poem that restores meaning for us.

Notes

1 Borges, Jorge Luis. Preface of FERVOR DE BUENOS AIRES by Jorge
   Luis Borges. Copyright © 1969 by Jorge Luis Borges, used by permission of
   The Wylie Agency LLC.
2 Novalis. *The Disciples at Saïs and Other Fragments*. London: Methuen &
   Co., 1903.
3 Minkowski, Eugène. *Verso una cosmologia. Frammenti filosofici [Towards
   a Cosmology: Philosophical Fragments]*. Italian translation. Turin:
   Einaudi, 2005. Also Bachelard, Gaston. *The Poetics of Space*. New York:
   Penguin Books, 2014, and Bollas, Christopher. *The Evocative Object
   World*. Abingdon and New York: Routledge/Taylor & Francis Group, 2009.
4 The concept of "reverberation" recalls, in some respects, the concept of an
   "objective correlative" sparked by T. S. Eliot and developed by Montale. In
   an essay (in *The Sacred Wood: Essays on Poetry and Criticism*; London:
   Methuen & Co. Ltd., 1920), T. S. Eliot defines it as "a series of objects, a
   situation, a chain of events ready to turn into the formula of a particular
   emotion" and arousing in the reader what the poet feels, without the need
   for explanation or particular mediations.
5 Penna, Sandro. "Mi nasconda la notte e il dolce vento [Night and Sweet
   Wind: Hide Me]," in *Poesie [Poems]*. Milan: Garzanti Editore, 1989.
6 Leopardi, Giacomo. "La sera del dì di festa [The Evening of the Feast
   Day]" in *Canti [Songs]*, edited by Ugo Dotti. Milan: Feltrinelli Editore,
   2008.
7 Penna, Sandro. "Mi nasconda la notte e il dolce vento [Night and Sweet
   Wind: Hide Me]" in *Poesie [Poems]*. Milan: Garzanti Editore, 1989.
8 Hillman, James. *Re-Visioning Psychology*. New York: Harper & Row, 1975.

9 Donne, John, "To His Mistress Going to Bed," in *The Complete Poetry and Selected Prose of John Donne*, edited by Charles M. Coffin. New York: Modern Library, 2001.

10 Byatt, A. S. "Observe the neurones: Between, above and below John Donne," *Times Literary Supplement*, Sept. 22, 2006. See also Byatt, A. S., "Feeling thought: Donne and the embodied mind," in *The Cambridge Companion to John Donne*, edited by Achsah Guibbory. Cambridge: Cambridge University Press, 2006, pp. 247–258.

11 Schrott, Raoul, and Jacobs, Arthur. *Gehirn und Gedicht. Wie wir unsere Wirklichkeit konstruieren [Brain and Poem. How We Construct our Reality]*. Monaco: Hanser Verlag, 2011.

12 Lingiardi, Vittorio. *La confusione è precisa in amore [Confusion is Precise in Love]*. Rome: Nottetempo, 2012.

13 "The Poets light but Lamps" in *The Poems of Emily Dickinson: Variorum Edition*, edited by Ralph W. Franklin, Cambridge, MA: The Belknap Press of Harvard University Press, Copyright © 1998 by the President and Fellows of Harvard College. Copyright © 1951, 1955 by the President and Fellows of Harvard College. Copyright © renewed 1979, 1983 by the President and Fellows of Harvard College. Copyright © 1914, 1918, 1919, 1924, 1929, 1930, 1932, 1935, 1937, 1942 by Martha Dickinson Bianchi. Copyright © 1952, 1957, 1958, 1963, 1965 by Mary L. Hampson. Used by permission. All rights reserved.

14 Bollas, Christopher. *Being a Character: Psychoanalysis and Self-Experience*. New York: Hill and Wang. London: Routledge, 1992.

15 See Chapter 3, Note 12.

16 Bollas, Christopher. *The Shadow of the Object*. London: Routledge, 2017, p. 15.

17 Bollas, Christopher. *Being a Character: Psychoanalysis and Self-Experience*. New York: Hill and Wang. London: Routledge, 1992.

18 Simic, Charles. "Note on Poetry and Philosophy," in *The Life of Images: Selected Prose*. New York: Ecco Press, 2015.

19 Heaney, Seamus. "The Sense of Place," in *Preoccupations*. London: Faber, 1980.

20 Bollas, Christopher. *Being a Character: Psychoanalysis and Self-Experience*. New York: Hill and Wang. London: Routledge, 1992.

21 Wordsworth, William. *The Prelude (Book I)*. London: Penguin Classics, 1996.

22 "The Angle of a Landscape," "By my Window have I for Scenery" in *The Poems of Emily Dickinson: Variorum Edition*, edited by Ralph W. Franklin, Cambridge, MA: The Belknap Press of Harvard University Press, Copyright © 1998 by the President and Fellows of Harvard College. Copyright © 1951, 1955 by the President and Fellows of Harvard College. Copyright © renewed 1979, 1983 by the President and Fellows of Harvard College. Copyright © 1914, 1918, 1919, 1924, 1929, 1930, 1932, 1935, 1937, 1942 by Martha Dickinson Bianchi. Copyright © 1952, 1957, 1958, 1963, 1965 by Mary L. Hampson. Used by permission. All rights reserved.

23 Frost, Robert. *Collected Poems of Robert Frost*. New York: Henry Holt and Company, 1939.

24 Frost, Robert. *Conversations on the Craft of Poetry*. New York: Holt, Rinehart, and Winston, 1961.

25 Ogden, Thomas. *Reverie and Interpretation. Sensing Something Human*, London and New York: Routledge, 1997.

26 Ogden, Thomas. "'The Music of What Happens' in Poetry and Psycho-analysis." *International Journal of Psychoanalysis* 80 (1999), p. 992.

27 Ammons, A. R. "A poem is a walk," *Epoch* 18 (1968), pp. 114–119.

28 Wallace, Stevens. "The Nobler Rider and the Sound of Words," in *The Necessary Angel: Essays on Reality and the Imagination*. London: Faber, 1960.

29 Recalcati, Massimo. *Jacques Lacan. Desiderio, godimento, soggettivazione [Jacques Lacan. Desire, Jouissance, Subjectification]*. Milan: Raffaello Cortina, 2012, pp. 271–278.

30 Baudelaire, Charles. "Correspondances [Correspondences]," in *Les Fleurs du mal [The Flowers of Evil]*. Paris: Larousse, 2011.

31 Rosselli, Amelia. "Variazioni belliche [War Variations]," in *Le poesie [The Poems]*. Milan: Garzanti, 2004.

32 Heaney, Seamus. *The Redress of Poetry: Oxford Lectures*. London: Faber and Faber Limited, 1995.

33 Frost, Robert. "The Figure a Poem Makes," in *Collected Poems of Robert Frost*. New York: Henry Holt and Company, 1939.

34 Churchwell, Sarah. "Secrets and lies: Plath, privacy, publication and Ted Hughes's birthday letters," *Contemporary Literature* 42, no. 1 (2001), pp. 102–148.

35 Hughes, Ted. "Daffodils," in *Birthday Letters*. London: Faber, 2002.

36 Char, René. "Paris is finished today," in *Furor & Mystery and Other Poems*. Translated and edited by Mary Ann Caws and Nancy Kline. Boston: Black Widow Press, 2010.

37 Frost, Robert. "The Most of It," in *A Witness Tree*. New York: Henry Holt and Company, 1942.

38 Rilke, Rainer Maria. *I sonetti a Orfeo [Sonnets to Orpheus]*. Italian translation in *Poesie [Poems]* (1908–1926), Vol. 2. Turin: Einaudi, 1995.

39 Stevens, Wallace. "Adagia," in *Opus Posthumous*. London: Faber, 1960.

40 Brief quote from p. 56 from *Johnny Panic and the Bible of Dreams* by Sylvia Plath. Copyright © 1960, 1965, 1971, 1981 by the Estate of Sylvia Plath. Used by permission of HarperCollins Publishers.

41 Ogden, Thomas. *Reclaiming Unlived Life: Experiences in Psychoanalysis*. London and New York: Routledge, 2016.

42 Rilke, Rainer Maria. *Le finestre [Windows]*. Italian translation in *Poesie [Poems] (1908–1926)*, Vol. 2. Turin: Einaudi, Torino 1995.

43 Bromberg, Philip. *Standing in the Spaces*. New York: Routledge, 1998.

44 "Keeping Things Whole" from *Selected Poems of Mark Strand* by Mark Strand, copyright © 1979, 1980 Mark Strand. Used by permission of Alfred A. Knopf, an imprint of the Knopf Doubleday Publishing Group, a division of Penguin Random House LLC. All rights reserved.

Chapter 11

The therapist as gardener

If you have a garden and a library, you have everything you need.

Cicero, *Letter to Varro*[1]

Nina Coltart, the legendary independent English psychoanalyst, declared "in an ideal world, all psychotherapists would have a garden." A garden, she said, would offer them "sources of psychic nourishment [...] that should *not* be concerned with analysis or therapy."[2] Coltart's advice refers to what she calls the survival of the psychoanalyst. I believe though that a therapist should have a garden because his or her talents are like the talents of a gardener, the "guardian of the unpredictable," and because a garden is a place of variety and patience, a "mental territory of hope."[3] Not to mention that each garden is different: each has its own personality, which we must not crush—its own geography and its own culture. An Italian-style garden is geometric and formal; a French one is symmetrical and sumptuous; an English one is more wild and less likely to present an overview; a Persian one is like a carpet—a fragrant microcosm with a central fountain like a navel. "Neither a flower nor a shadow," said Barthes about a Japanese garden. "Where is the human? In the carrying of rocks, in the furrows of the raking, in the work of writing."[4]

A garden, too, is a landscape. Foucault said that it's "the smallest particle and at the same time the total of the world."[5] A garden is a typical case of "heterotopia," a place where many imaginary spaces coexist; it is a mythical and real contestation of the space in which we live. Like an island or an oasis, and like a cemetery (which is the garden of the dead), it has the magical aspect of all spaces that are separate and enclosed.

DOI: 10.4324/9781003252979-11

You could use a garden to tell the story of humans (and of course the story of animals too). You could start from the Songs of Songs, where the body/garden—sensual and religious—is the main character: "Let my beloved come into his garden / and eat its exquisite fruits." Or you could start even earlier, from the most famous garden of all, *ēden*—a Hebrew word meaning "place of delights," or "countryside," or, in other traditions, "place in which much water flows." A place from which we were driven out; a place that seems to embody the fantasies of an ideal landscape that we encountered in Chapter 5 (and after all, don't people exult that a wonderful vacation spot is "an earthly paradise"?).

"Heaven on earth, paradise on earth," muttered Pia Pera. "Kafka wrote somewhere that there we should wonder not why man has lost earthly paradise, but why man does not try to return to it. As a citizen of Prague, perhaps he failed to see that anyone who goes back to the countryside—anyone who wants their own garden for himself—is driven by this desire for a return to Eden."[6] And that's a handmade Eden, which permits us to (in exchange for a lot of effort) contain the chaos and benevolently "cheat the laws of nature."[7] Not because a garden is "unnatural" but because it is, to a certain degree, malleable matter, controllable matter. Like almost everything else, a garden is both nature and culture. Kant includes the art of the garden in his chapter on painting:

Painting [...] I would divide into the art of beautifully portraying nature and that of beautifully composing its products. The first would be painting proper, the second would be gardening [... The latter] is nothing more than the embellishment of the soil by means of that same variety that nature offers to intuition (lawns, flowers, bushes and trees, and also the waters, hills and valleys), but combined differently and in accordance with certain ideas.[8]

Il faut cultiver notre jardin, said Voltaire.[9] Voltaire was himself a gardener, and the metaphor of the garden is crucial in his *Candide*. The novella has the Baron's garden, from which Candide and Cunégonde are, like Adam and Eve, expelled; it also has the El Dorado garden, as the imaginary second-best option; and—finally—it has the garden to cultivate, the garden of reality. We go from fiction (aesthetic and botanical) to reality, via idealization. (In Leonard Bernstein's operetta version, "Candide," just doing the best we can.)[10] If everyone cultivates his own garden, we will have "our garden," a garden of humanity, where all people can enjoy the individual plants. A Utopia that is enlightened and, oxymoronically, pragmatic, Candide's garden is a possible good world, also during the analytic enterprise.

While Nina Coltart considers that a garden supports the therapist's own survival, others propose a manifesto of botanical survival with a bit of irony.[11] Indeed it's impossible to avoid making fun of gardening trends and their inevitable implications about society and character: a gardener obsessing over rare plants, or being fanatical about a symmetrical and orderly layout (as if the garden were a closet full of clothing), or intolerant of an unacceptably trivial domestic shrub, or the disreputable look of fallen leaves on the lawn. And, finally: the love of greenery can deliver pleasant surprises: a small balcony—in the shadow of looming cement towers—that nevertheless brims with carefully tended flowers is more touching than a luxurious *Miltonia spectabilis* orchid.

Gardens are always a good way to get to know other people (for example, in the array of garden types in Berlin's Gardens of the World park) and to get to know oneself, because a home garden always resembles its gardener. And since nothing escapes the notice of psychologists, I see a steady stream of scientific publications flowing in, from England and from New Zealand: "'My garden is an expression of me': Exploring householders' relationships with their gardens" and "Landscapes of the lifespan: Exploring accounts of own gardens and gardening," which study not only the identity aspects of gardening but the therapeutic aspects of gardening as well.[12]

In the charter of the International Committee for Historic Gardens, drawn up in Florence in 1982, I read these articles:

Article 2: "The historic garden is an architectural composition whose constituents are primarily vegetal and therefore living, which means that they are perishable and renewable." Thus its appearance reflects the perpetual balance between the cycle of the seasons, the growth and decay of nature and the desire of the artist and craftsman to keep it permanently unchanged.

Article 5: As the expression of the direct affinity between civilisation and nature, and as a place of enjoyment suited to meditation or repose, the garden thus acquires the cosmic significance of an idealised image of the world, a "paradise" in the etymological sense of the term, and yet a testimony to a culture, a style, an age, and often to the originality of a creative artist.

The garden is therefore a living work of plant life but also, inevitably, animal and mineral life. Anyone who has spent a day in a garden—strolling, reading or conversing—knows what I am talking about. A person could know this even as a kid—if she was a city kid lucky enough to be taken to the park, or if he grew up in the country with a vegetable garden out back.

Abandoned gardens are beautiful. There was one near the seaside house on the Ligurian coast where I spent my childhood vacations: we were forbidden to go into it. How wonderful it was to disobey!—to wait for sunset and then sneak in there with my friends, to explore (frightened, but enchanted) the "briars had mounted toward the trees," the branches that crawled on the ground but then went back up "to meet what expands in the air," the interweaving of "brambles, branches, leaves, fibres, tufts, twigs, tendrils, and thorns" of that garden that was "as impenetrable as a forest, as populous as a city, as rustling as a nest, as dark as a cathedral, as fragrant as a bouquet, as solitary as a tomb, and as lively as a crowd."[13]

A vast gallery of paintings, drawings, letters, stories, novels, and films tell us all that a garden can be. Pissarro's intimate corners; Klimt's meadows; *Elective Affinities* and *The Garden of the Finzi-Continis*; *The Draughtsman's Contract* and *Edward Scissorhands*. And then there is *Sido*, who made the garden into *a room of her own*:

> Where did she get so much authority, so much substance, she who didn't even leave her neighborhood three times in a year? Where did she get that gift of defining, of penetrating, and the pontifical form of her observations?[14]

…and passed on to her daughter, Colette, her love of nature and her art of cultivating: cultivating the earth, and children, and lovers, and writing.

> I would return when the bell rang for the first Mass, but only after […] I had tasted the water of the two hidden springs which I worshiped […]. The first spring tasted of oak leaves, the second of iron

and hyacinth stalks. Every time I talk about them, I hope that my mouth will be full of their flavor when my time comes, and that I can carry away with me that imaginary sip.[15]

The variety of a garden is not limited to just the type and number of its plants or its style. There are also all the different ways it can be used: for prayer, for meditation, for refuge; as a hiding place, as a love nest, or as a den for quickie sex. Because it's a location that's set apart—because it might have a bench—it can be suitable for intimate conversation, for moments of sincerity and surrender. It's a psychological setting that's set apart, that has rules to be respected, with cures on offer and freedoms to be discovered.

At least that's how the *locus amoenus* appears, in the mind's eye, in a Platonic dialogue: a grove shaded by a large plane tree and refreshed by a spring—not a garden, but a place nevertheless suitable for bringing together thought, conversation, and landscape.

Phaedrus: Do you see that tall plane tree?
Socrates: How not?
Phaedrus: There is shade and a gentle breeze, and grass if we want to sit, or lie down.[16]

At the opposite extreme, and thus akin to it, is the *locus horridus*— Dante's dark woods or a fairytale forest—which inspires all kinds of fears and is a place of loss, danger, and initiation.

And gloomy foliage in the bottom
of the woods, of the only woods,
of the eternal forest; they make me live
they storm me in a thousand
different gloomy choruses.[17]

Then, here, under "another sky" and "another sunlight," are the gentle and enchanted spaces: "The little forest, whose evergreen leaf," "the brightest garden / never touched by frost," "please, brother, come into *my* garden."

Emily Dickinson was 14 years old when she asked a friend if she happened to collect flowers and plants for an herbarium: "It would be such a treasure."[18] She held a rose along with a book in the childhood portrait of her by painter Otis A. Bullard, and she never lost her love of nature: gardens, flowers, and the seasons were to become essential presences in her poetry. *Her* garden was like a beach on which the summer sea deposits its verses:

My Garden—like the Beach—
Denotes there be—a Sea—
That's Summer—
Such as These—the Pearls
She fetches—such as Me.[19]

But in one sharp and poignant work, she writes: "I hav'nt told my garden yet, / Lest that should conquer me; / I have not quite the strength now / To break it to the bee."[20] There comes a time when even the gardener dies, despite an old adage saying that "from a rose's point of view, a gardener is immortal."

I Have Not Told My Garden Yet is the line from the Amherst poet that Pia Pera chose as the title for her final book, before she disappeared "into the enigma." She had for a while been part of the eternal present of her garden near the town of Lucca—part of that "fluctuating world of continuous transformations." She knew she was being ravaged, deep down, like a plant ravaged by bad weather; that she was "drying up, withering, losing pieces, and—above all—not moving as I would like."[21] She tended her garden to the very end. Then, progressively—as her motor neuron disease progressed—she watched as other trusted hands tended her garden. Readying herself to meet "Christ the gardener,"[22] she wrote a book about gardens and about dying, and about being the gardener of oneself and of the world. She upended the perspective: seeds as thoughts and thoughts as seeds.

Reluctantly, I'm getting close to the end of my walk though all these gardens, and I am picturing a favorite image of mine: the possibly unintentional photograph of the shadow of Claude Monet's head on the surface of the water lily pond in his garden at Giverny. I consider this moving self-portrait to be the aquatic embodiment of the genius who painted the water lily cycle—those 250 paintings, many of them shaped by his cataract-clouded vision. That cloudiness is the subject of Lisel Mueller's poem, "Monet Refuses the Operation." In this ode to blurry sight, Monet's vision is not an obstacle but rather a doorway to new possibilities; after a whole lifetime, the painter has finally managed to perceive the glow of a street lamp as an angel, and to learn that the horizon is not a dividing line—that sky and water are one.[23]

Monet's hat floats in the water like the flowers he painted a thousand times with ever-changing reflections. His water lilies, immersed in the pond and "blooming in the sky,"[24] are a landscape that he pursued all his life. The most profound and mysterious example of a *mindscape* when it shines with meaning.

Notes

1 Cicero. Letter to Varro, in *Ad Familiares IX*, 4.
2 Coltart, Nina. *How to Survive as a Psychotherapist*. Lanham, MD: Aronson, 1993, p. 98.
3 Clément, Gilles, *Il giardino in movimento [The Garden in Motion]*. Italian translation, Macerata: Quodlibet, 2011. Clément, G. *Il giardiniere planetario ["The Planetary Garden" and Other Writings]*. Italian translation, Milan: 22 Publishing, 2008 [2004].
4 Barthes, Roland. *L'impero dei segni [Empire of Signs]*. Italian translation, Turin: Einaudi, 1974.
5 Foucault, Michel. "Eterotopie," ["Heterotopia"] in *Archivio Foucault 3. Interventi, colloqui, interviste [Foucault Archive 3. Interventions, Talks, Interviews]*. Italian translation, Milan: Feltrinelli, 1998.
6 Pera, Pia. *L'orto di un perdigiorno. Confessioni di un apprendista ortolano [The Garden of a Layabout. Confessions of an Apprentice Vegetable Gardener]*. Milan: Ponte alle Grazie, 2003.
7 Grimal, Pierre. *L'arte dei giardini. Una breve storia [The Art of Gardens. A Brief History]*. Italian translation, Milan: Feltrinelli, 1994.
8 Kant, Immanuel. *Critica della capacità di giudizio [Critique of Pure Reason]*, Vol. 2. Italian translation, Milan: Rizzoli, 1995.
9 Voltaire, *Candide*, 1759.
10 Bernstein, Leonard. "Make Our Garden Grow," in *Candide*. New York: Macmillan, 1976.
11 Pasti, Umberto. *Giardini e no. Manuale di sopravvivenza botanica [Gardens and Not. Botanical Survival Manual]*. Milan: Bompiani, 2010.
12 Gross, Harriet, and Lane, Nicola. "Landscapes of the lifespan: Exploring accounts of own gardens and gardening," *Journal of Environmental Psychology* 27, no. 3 (2007), pp. 225–241. Freeman, Claire, Dickinson, Katharine J. M., Porter, Stefan, and Van Heezik, Yolanda. "'My garden is an expression of me': Exploring householders' relationships with their gardens," *Journal of Environmental Psychology* 32, no. 2 (2012), pp. 135–143.
13 Hugo, Victor. *Les Misérables*, 1862.
14 Colette. *Sido*, 1929.
15 Colette. *Sido*, 1929.

16 Plato, *Phaedrus*, c. 370 BC.

17 Zanzotto, Andrea. "IX Ecloghe [IX Eclogues]." In *Poesie e prose scelte [Selected Poems and Prose]*. Milan: Mondadori, 1999. Copyright © The Estate of Andrea Zanzotto. Published by arrangement with The Italian Literary Agency.

18 *The Letters of Emily Dickinson*, edited by Thomas H. Johnson, Associate Editor, Theodora Ward, Cambridge, MA: The Belknap Press of Harvard University Press, Copyright © 1958 by the President and Fellows of Harvard College. Copyright © renewed 1986 by the President and Fellows of Harvard College. Copyright © 1914, 1924, 1932, 1942 by Martha Dickinson Bianchi. Copyright © 1952 by Alfred Leete Hampson. Copyright © 1960 by Mary L. Hampson. Used by permission. All rights reserved.

19 "My Garden—like the Beach" in *The Poems of Emily Dickinson: Variorum Edition*, edited by Ralph W. Franklin, Cambridge, MA: The Belknap Press of Harvard University Press, Copyright © 1998 by the President and Fellows of Harvard College. Copyright © 1951, 1955 by the President and Fellows of Harvard College. Copyright © renewed 1979, 1983 by the President and Fellows of Harvard College. Copyright © 1914, 1918, 1919, 1924, 1929, 1930, 1932, 1935, 1937, 1942 by Martha Dickinson Bianchi. Copyright © 1952, 1957, 1958, 1963, 1965 by Mary L. Hampson. Used by permission. All rights reserved.

20 "I hav'nt told my garden yet" in *The Poems of Emily Dickinson: Variorum Edition*, edited by Ralph W. Franklin, Cambridge, MA: The Belknap Press of Harvard University Press, Copyright © 1998 by the President and Fellows of Harvard College. Copyright © 1951, 1955 by the President and Fellows of Harvard College. Copyright © renewed 1979, 1983 by the President and Fellows of Harvard College. Copyright © 1914, 1918, 1919, 1924, 1929, 1930, 1932, 1935, 1937, 1942 by Martha Dickinson Bianchi. Copyright © 1952, 1957, 1958, 1963, 1965 by Mary L. Hampson. Used by permission. All rights reserved.

21 Pera, Pia. *Al giardino ancora non l'ho detto [I Hav'nt Told my Garden Yet]*. Milan: Ponte alle Grazie, 2016.

22 In the Gospel of John (20:15), when the resurrected Christ appears to Mary Magdalene, she fails to recognize him—she thinks he is the keeper of the garden. This episode was depicted in numerous paintings (by Fra Angelico, Bronzino, Tintoretto, Poussin, and others), with Christ almost always shown carrying a shovel and wearing a sun-hat.

23 Mueller, Lisel. "Monet Refuses the Operation," in *Second Language*. Baton Rouge, LA: Louisiana State University Press, 1986.

24 Proust, Marcel. *À la recherche du temps perdu: Du côté de chez Swann [In Search of Lost Time: Swann's Way]*, 1913.

Chapter 12

Dis-oriented

The westerner in me was discomposed.

Joseph Conrad, *Under Western Eyes*[1]

The term "orienting" means "to turn toward the east"; the sense of orientation is the ability to recognize the cardinal points of a compass. There are four cardinal directions, and they mix in infinite gradations. We say "orientation" for spatial orientation, or for sexual, professional, or political orientation: it has to do with being in the world and knowing one's own positions. Positions that one can lose and then find again. Orientation is established on the basis of the cardinal points and thus of the sun's path, the direction of the shadows, the position of the stars. Birds of prey orient themselves visually; bats orient themselves acoustically; certain insects orient themselves by chemical clues; mammals usually rely on their sense of smell. A competent human being will do orientation by mixing these different sensory components with some cognitive operations. And humans build instruments: maps, sextants, compasses, and GPS (the satellite-based global positioning system).

On a surface terrain, the cardinal points indicate the four main directions in which one can move: north, south, east, west. I read that these names derive from a German myth recounting that in ancient times, four dwarfs held up the sky: Norðri (North), Suðri (South), Austri (East), and Vestri (West). Here in Italy, the terms come—instead—from Latin, and they enlighten us about the direction of the sun: the sun rises in the east (*oriente*, from *oriri*, "to rise"), and in the west it heads down (*occidente*, from *occident*, "going down"). For south, we Italians say *meridione*, which alludes to the middle of the day; and for the north we

DOI: 10.4324/9781003252979-12

say *settentrione*, referring to the Latin *septem triones*, the seven oxen towing the Plough constellation across the night sky; the Plough (or "Big Dipper" in America) that points a navigator northward. Amid those four orthogonal points are four other intermediate points (northeast, southeast, etc.) and in among *those* are another eight points. And then there is the wind rose, showing where the different winds blow in from: here in Italy, we have the *tramontana* from the north, the *grecale* from the north-east, the *sirocco* from the south-east, and so on.

Just a few pieces of information suffice to convey the enormous landscape power of the cardinal points. Before asking myself how vivid they still are, I try to dig for them among my memories, the memories of a child who played "Person, Place, Thing," and in my own imagination as a white man, as a northern-Italian adult who was born at the end of Italy's economic boom. This helps to remind me that the landscape "is not nature," but is always "culture projected onto mountains, oceans, forests, volcanoes and deserts."[2]

The *North* for me means cold; snow; mountains (even when I'm in southern mountains); upward thrust; Flemish painting; bears; reindeer; herring; conifers; steppes; Saint Petersburg; the Fær Øer Islands; fjords; raspberries; Laplanders; bundling up in woolens; Wagner; Mann; Bergman; the Snow Queen. And it means the solemn Tranströmer, who writes that the north is where the true lynx lives, with its sharp claws and its dreaming eyes.[3] And the northern skies that surprised Manganelli on his travels, "accustomed" as he was "to a yolk-like sun, a hen-like sun, an animal sun."[4]

The *South* for me means warmth; sun; swimming; airy clothing; *Carmen*, caper bushes growing over stone ruins; the Mediterranean; the Sahara. And Gide, who writes: "This southern sky torments me like a frame of impossible happiness."[5] But it also means South America; Patagonia; and Tierra del Fuego and Antarctica: "The deepest and most radical of the Souths, an icy South."[6]

For me the *East* means dawn; the Middle East and the Far East; Salgari's adventure fantasies; Kipling; *Madame Butterfly*; *Turandot*; *Apocalypse Now*; Mishima; the Dalai Lama; martial arts; Zen; feng shui; haiku; samurai; Zen gardens; manga; Yasujirō Ozu's films; and the Ganges. And it means Baudelaire, who writes: "Languid Asia and burning Africa."[7] And Edward Said, too:

> there was (and is) a linguistic Orient, a Freudian Orient, a Spenglerian Orient, a Darwinian Orient, a racist Orient—and so on. Yet never

has there been such a thing as a pure, or unconditional, Orient; similarly, never has there been a nonmaterial form of Orientalism, much less something so innocent as an "idea" of the Orient.[8]

For me the *West* means the sunset; the Far West; Redskins; cowboys; Puccini again—but this time it's the *Fanciulla del West*; Tex Willer; the Pilgrims; the American dream; Mormons; Anabaptists; Methodists; Hollywood; New York (although the East Coast has its own East Side). And it means Kerouac, who wrote that he was pulled westward through the darkness he could see in the city nearby.[9]

But do the cardinal points still live on in us? Is there any value to these disseminations of mine—so full of contradictions and prejudices? Do the cardinal points still chart a course? Do they orient the psyche? Are they the personal and narrowly idiosyncratic tools of a literary voyager, or are they still recognizable as "cultural absolutes"? What place in my head is held by Lawrence of Arabia's orientalized Middle East?—and Edward Said's demythologized Middle East?—and Joseph Massad's post-colonial Middle East?[10] What about the Middle East of the Gaza Strip and that of the jihadist executions? The gilded Mediterranean of my adolescence, and the Mediterranean of the people-smugglers and their shipwrecked, drowning refugees?

A few months ago, I dreamed of Palmyra, which I visited when I was 20 years old: but what place did I dream of? Was it the ancient "bride of the desert," or was it the place where ISIS executioners beheaded the elderly director of the archaeological site? What remains of a place's identity when bombs erase the territory and its young people take off for unknown countries that they might never reach? What is the role of memory, and what are its reconfigurations in an era of global warfare?[11]

The cardinal points contain the imaginal fullness of an archetype, but also its unmoving rigidity. An indispensable link to our imaginary, which influences our style; but it would be dangerous—inadvisable—to identify oneself with it in a unilateral way. Radicalizing the cardinal points makes us repetitive and entrenched. Pretending that they do not exist suspends us in eternal fluctuations.

Envoi is a poem by Octavio Paz with a particular history: it appears, in various languages, in books and cultural projects addressing the political construction of spaces. It seems to tell the story of the orientation quadrants, their constraints and their potential, from within a jail whose walls correspond to the four cardinal points—the North is not-knowing, the South is a landscape not yet invented, the East is mirror and the West is stony silence.[12]

I believe that despite everything, we are body-maps. We understand this when we read even just a few lines of this poem by John Donne,[13] who orients his body in illness:

Whilst my physicians by their love are grown
Cosmographers, and I their map, who lie
Flat on this bed, that by them may be shown
That this is my south-west discovery,
Per fretum febris, by these straits to die,

I joy, that in these straits I see my west;
For, though their currents yield return to none,
What shall my west hurt me? As west and east
In all flat maps (and I am one) are one,
So death doth touch the resurrection.

Is the Pacific Sea my home? Or are
The eastern riches? Is Jerusalem?
Anyan, and Magellan, and Gibraltar,
All straits, and none but straits, are ways to them,
Whether where Japhet dwelt, or Cham, or Shem.

Or we understand it when we read the psycho-geographical experiment of Madeleine de Scudéry, the Précieuse,[14] who in 1654 began to draw a map to accompany her novel *Clélie*. She needed the map to define her protagonist's emotional paths. Her "*Carte de Tendre*" was a map of the land of tenderness, i.e., an imaginary map, whose shape vaguely resembles a uterus. It was a map-landscape for orienting oneself during an affective journey: these plains and trees, a river, a lake, a few cities, a sea (*la mer dangereuse*) tell of an itinerary in which emotions take on topographical form. The starting place is called New Friendship, and a river runs through it, called Inclination. Just before the river's mouth, two other tributary streams come in; on the left is "Recognition" and on the right is "Esteem." The two rivers flow into the Dangerous Sea, and the shore beyond that sea is called the Unknown Land. The sea represents passion: it is full of rocky obstacles that block the way. On the left bank of the river Inclination are two roads, one good and one bad. The bad road passes through the territories of Indiscretion, Perfidy, Malice, and Pride, and then ends at the sea of Enmity. The good road passes through Complacency, Submission, Pampering, Assiduity, Readiness, Sensitivity, Tenderness, Obedience, and Constant Friendship, and then arrives at Tenderness on Recognition (*Tendre sur Reconnaissance*). Unlike the other maps, Madeleine de Scudéry's map involves an intimate exploration of place-affects. Moving through that territory means immersing oneself in an emotional geography. For her era, it was an enterprise that was revolutionary as well as playful: from a female viewpoint, it narrated intellectual relationships, friendship, love, and sexuality. An invented map that invented a subjectivity.[15]

I hope that today's maps in the psychoanalytic field are capable of considering all the elements that emerge from contemporary landscapes: migration and disorientation, but also invention and fruitfulness.[16] "Geographies of psychoanalysis" is the name that Lorena Preta chose, a few years ago, for a project promoting the study of the "fertile contaminations" that seep in when psychoanalysis steps outside its (sometimes narrow) geographical and cultural boundaries.

A South Wind—has a pathos
Of individual Voice—
As One detect on Landings
An Emigrant's address.

A Hint of Ports and Peoples—
And much not understood—
The fairer—for the farness—
And for the foreignhood.[17]

It is not only a matter of dialoguing with other disciplines; it's also about encountering other anthropological positions, other geographical quadrants. Observing how psychoanalysis behaves as it moves away from the Western womb that generated it. A psychoanalysis that can sustain the tension among all the spaces that surround it and inhabit it: the restlessness of the heterotopias, the traps (but also the advantages) of virtual realities, the anonymity of non-places, the uncertainty of random urban landscapes, the nostalgia of the Grand Tour, the ruins of antiquity and the wreckage of contemporaneity, the migrations that are laden with the dead but that also carry new lives—for people who are fleeing war and can flourish elsewhere.

As a Jewish refugee fleeing the Nazis, Walter Benjamin reached the French/Spanish border and—in exhaustion—committed suicide. The Gestapo had seized his house in Paris, his whole library. He had just survived a long climb over the mountains to cross the border. Up ahead he had a journey to America, where an unknown new life awaited him. By the cemetery in the border town of Portbou (where he was purportedly buried), the Israeli sculptor Dani Karavan created *Passagen*, a monument in the landscape whose name refers to Benjamin's unfinished work, *Passagenwerk*. A walled-in metal staircase leads steeply down toward the Mediterranean, but then comes a thick glass barrier. Inscribed on it is a fragment of Benjamin's writing: "It is a more arduous task to honour the memory of anonymous beings than that of famous persons. The construction of history is consecrated to the memory of those who have no name."

Benjamin had written that it takes "a certain amount of practice to get lost [in a city] as one gets lost in a forest." It is a practice that teaches that "the street names should speak to the wanderer like the creaking of dry branches" and the narrow streets of the center city "must mark the hours of the day just as a mountain valley does."[18] Benjamin says that he was late to learn it, but he traces it back to the labyrinths that decorated the blotting papers of his notebooks—no—he traces it back even earlier: to the *Tiergarten*, to the places of his Berlin childhood.

Without an internalized link to the origin of our landscape, we risk not just getting lost, but being lost, if it's true that "we are lost when there is no object of desire; and we make ourselves lost when there is an object of desire."[19] Losing our bearings can pitch us into disarray, can confuse the dawn for the sunset; but not knowing how to get lost impoverishes the imagination, precludes discovery, curbs abandonment. Cardinal points must be lost and found again. Dis-orienting oneself, "breaking apart and reformulating" (in the Latin motto of the long-ago alchemists: *solve et coagula*), leads to a final volatile intoxication that— once again—our Emily Dickinson captured best, with expert candor:

The Wind took up the Northern Things
And piled them in the south—
Then gave the East unto the West
And opening his mouth

The four Divisions of the Earth
Did make as to devour
[...]
How intimate, a Tempest past
The Transport of the Bird—[20]

After a long analysis with me, a patient writes me a letter that ends like this: "The sky above and around my block yesterday was extraordinarily full/empty of clouds and sunshine. This, at least, might have pleased us both—although for opposite reasons. You are always my Southeast." I ended my reply to this letter with:

> The cardinal points are an invented thing and also a true thing, which helps in orientation. You're right. Perhaps the lines that link two people who have done an analytical journey together end up at a point that's virtual and very strong—a *cardinal* point. And then there is the sky, which is always full/empty of clouds and sunshine; a sky that we both like, and a sky under which we both shall live.

Knowing how to orient oneself in psychoanalysis means exploring more closely the spaces between the cardinal points; contemplating the vastness of geographies that are relational, amorous and spiritual; learning to travel to different psychic latitudes, trying to negotiate the inevitable conflicts; imagining cardinal points that can contain each other and can point us toward a south within the north, an east within the west. And building new maps.

In an age increasingly devoted to the self-soothing tending of one's own little garden—while the shared landscape gets disfigured by buildings plastered with billboards or locales that have been beaten into obedience and residential tameness—the concept of a "Third landscape" is useful to us from a psychic point of view as well. In the urban void, observes Gilles Clément,[21] grass, shrubs, and flowers appear: small primordial forests of abandonment. Not infrequently, the inhabitants feel concern or disdain when they see this resurgent nature, this zombie nature—because of its wild and even somewhat "borderline" appearance. Clément, a landscape architect, an agricultural engineer, a botanist and entomologist, considers the biodiversity found in these places to be a resource of diversity and beauty. The Third landscape idea touches not just cities, of course, but also roads, heaths, bogs, river-banks, and places that are to some degree uncertain: the "undefined fragments" of the Planetary Garden which represent the sum of spaces abandoned by humankind, where nature takes control again.

The residual dimension of the Third landscape lies before us as a "grey zone." A space that speaks of social precariousness and individual stress, a no-man's land where we come across "the new poverty; immigrants; the marginalized; the excluded."[22] For this reason, perhaps, a poet is among the first to feel this landscape:

> Some flowers, like the sunchoke, that don't give a hoot, sprout up in the most devastated places, on the edge of major roads and in the floodplains that hate gardens and fences. They represent the liberating force that nature possesses, which at a certain moment produces—even in degraded places—something truly marvelous: a thing that wants nothing more than to be there, and once it has completed its passage, it leaves in perpetual metamorphosis.[23]

The Third landscape is the privileged space that welcomes the non-cultivated and contrasts with any anthropized territories subjected to human management and exploitation. In this category I would also include many nature parks that humans have—with the best of intentions?—cut off from any possible physical experience, transforming them into Disneyland-reserves or into areas for naturalistic voyeurism.

Following Baudrillard's simulacrum theory—the idea that capitalist consumerism has replaced reality with representations of reality—Jonathan Franzen, during a trip to Africa, has these considerations:

> It's impossible to escape the contrast between East Africa's clean and lushly vegetated parks, teeming with wildebeests and elephants, and the overgrazed, overpopulated, trash-strewn countrysides that separate them, the hegemony of Coca-Cola, the heavily guarded Del Monte pineapple plantations, the rail lines and highways that Chinese engineers are building to speed the extraction of soda ash and coal, the specters of AIDS and Islamic terrorism. The parks function as simulacra in which tourists, most of them white, all of them affluent, can "experience" an "Africa" whose representation is contingent on their money. The baobabs and the acacias are native, and at night the

southern constellations are unfamiliar to northerners; this much is genuine. But, in the same way that people in a real blizzard now exclaim that it looks just like a blizzard in a movie, you may find yourself viewing zebras in the Serengeti and recalling the zebras in a safari park in Florida. Not only is the real thing not real, it strikes you as a copy of a copy.[24]

In 1958, the situationist Guy Debord coined the term *psychogeography* to refer to the study of the effects of the geographical environment on an individual's affective behavior. Today, psychogeography seems destined to rigid distinctions among places: the areas that have been cosmetically-commercially embalmed (gentrified historic town centers; prettified villages); areas of globalized pseudo-aesthetics that are organized according to census groupings (from *ethnochic* to *ethnopop*); areas of social desertification that have been abandoned because of poverty, migration, or war.

The spirit of a place, the *genius loci*, is a collective and individual concept that gets built over time around relationships among people, objects, and landscapes. Marc Augé upended this simple notion in the 1990s and arrived at the concept of a non-place—the exact opposite of an anthropological place. A product of our post-modernity, a non-place is an "immense parenthesis"[25] destined to open up more and more: spaces devoid of any connotations (neither identity nor history)—commercial centers, highways, airports, international hotels. Their function is to promote consumption, homogenization, and the acceleration of travel. Places that leave no trace, Benjamin would say; places that are therefore irreconcilable with living. Indeed, refugee camps and immigration centers are also non-places: enormous (often deteriorating) waiting rooms for bewildered women and men who are lost between their place of origin and the place they're fated to go next.

Space has to do with power. Michel Foucault never tired of telling us this. With his concept of *heterotopia* he indicated "those spaces that have the particular characteristic of being connected to all other spaces, but in such a way as to suspend, neutralize, or reverse the set of the relationships that they themselves designate, reflect, or mirror."[26] A mirror is a heterotopia, Foucault says (with a mirror, we are where we are not), as is a *cemetery* ("the other city in which every family possesses its black abode"), a *theater*, a *cinema*, and a *garden* (which allow us to superimpose different incompatible locations on one single place), a *train*, a *boarding school*, a *Turkish bath*, a *bordello*, a *summer camp*, a *prison*, and a *mental hospital* (all of them based on a "system of opening and closure" that isolates them while also making them penetrable). And so, while utopias are "consoling," heterotopias are "disquieting."[27]

Already back in 1967, Foucault thought that, while the 19th century's great obsession had been history (and therefore time), the present epoch "could instead be considered the epoch of space," an epoch "of the simultaneous," "of juxtaposition," "of the close juxtaposition," "of the near and the far," "of the side-by-side," "of the dispersed." He had already understood that we live in a "moment in which the world experiences itself more as a great path that develops in time, as a network that crosses points and weaves its skein." Nowadays it is crucial to understand the relationship between spaces and flows, "placeless place" and "timeless time."[28] Not only integrated global networks, but also exiles, migrations, exoduses.

This is a decisive issue not only for the disciplines that focus on space and place (architecture, geography, environmental sciences, ecology and—I hope—politics), but also for psychoanalysis, which is guilty of having neglected the soul of places—and which will die if it does not keep a window open on the world.[29]

If psychoanalysis is "a dictionary of all the ways in which we can travel without ever arriving,"[30] how then can one orient oneself? Perhaps with a poem, like the one written by poet and immunologist Miroslav Holub. It is titled *Brief Reflection on Maps*, and it is a story about the power of maps and their ability to build roads along with us. In the poem, a scouting party of soldiers went missing in an Alpine snowstorm. The young lieutenant who had sent them out to scout was very worried; he feared they would not return. But one morning they appeared: one of them had found a map in his pocket. So what if it was a map of the Pyrenees and not the Alps?[31]

Giorgio Agamben recounts having glued maps of various cities together, for fun, thus composing a kind of big city "in which an alley in Rome opens onto a square in Paris, and a Parisian boulevard ends in a small Berlin street, and so on."[32] Cartography, he says, is the most interesting (or perhaps the most possible) way to think of a biography—of the relationship between a life and its places.

We know that the map is not a territory. The "extraordinary map" is us; it is a mental landscape that provides us with a sense of orientation... without telling us where we are. Life as a fantastic topography.

Notes

1 Conrad, Joseph. *Under Western Eyes*. New York: Harper & Brothers, 1911.
2 Bodei, Remo. *Paesaggi sublimi. L'uomo di fronte alla natura selvaggia [Sublime Landscapes. Man in the Face of Wilderness]*. Milan: Bompiani, 2008, p. 18.
3 Tranströmer, Tomas. *Storia fantastica [The Sailor's Yarn]* in *Poesie del silenzio [Poems of Silence]*. Italian translation. Milan: Crocetti, 2011.
4 Manganelli, Giorgio. *L'isola pianeta e altri settentrioni [The Island Planet and other Norths]*. Milan: Adelphi, 2006, p. 114.
5 André Gide writing to his friend Marc Drouin. See Lenstringant, F. *André Gide l'inquiéteur*, Vol. I: *Le ciel sur la terre ou l'inquiétude partagée [André Gide the Worrier, Vol. I: Heaven on Earth or Shared Anxiety] (1869–1918)*. Paris: Flammarion, 2011.
6 Del Giudice, Daniele, *Orizzonte mobile [Mobile Horizon]*. Turin: Einaudi, 2009, p. 3.
7 Baudelaire, Charles. "La chevelure [The Hair]," in *Les Fleurs du Mal [The Flowers of Evil]*. Paris: Larousse, 2011.
8 Said, Edward. *Orientalism*. London: Routledge & Kegan Paul, 1978.
9 Kerouac, Jack. *On the Road*. New York: Viking Press, 1957.
10 Joseph Massad, in *Desiring Arabs* (Chicago: University of Chicago Press, 2007), takes up and develops Edward Said's concept of "Orientalism" in terms of "sexual colonialism" (understood as exporting the "LGBT model" to non-Western countries). For Said, Orientalism was a constellation of false assumptions, often expressed in romantic forms, that reflected the attitude of Westerners toward Eastern populations and that justified an essentially colonial attitude toward Asia and the Middle East. Said also denounced the internalization—by the economic élite of the Arab world—of American and British ideas about Arab culture.
11 De Cesari, Chiara. *Transnational Memory*. Berlin: De Gruyter, 2014.
12 Paz, Octavio. "Envoi," in *The Production of Space* by Henri Lefebvre. Translated by Donald Nicholson-Smith. Oxford: Basil Blackwell, 1991.
13 Donne, John. "Hymn to God, My God, in My Sickness," in *The Complete Poetry and Selected Prose of John Donne*, edited by Charles M. Coffin. New York: Modern Library, 2001.
14 *Préciosité*, a 17th century women's movement that was mocked by Molière in his play *Les précieuses ridicules*, arose as a reaction to the coarseness of the men of Henry IV's court and in the Fronde. Their "salons" and "conversations" were the arena where the female experience of preciousness developed. The *précieuses* group owed its privilege to the existence of this

zone suspended between reality and fiction, a private friendship space for experimentation, where the chosen few learned to look after themselves and consider themselves as deserving of happiness. Asserting the value of emotions and sensitivity, the *précieuse* model was a manifesto of cultural opposition to male forms of power.

15 Bruno, Giuliana. "Atlante delle emozioni [Atlas of Emotions]," in *Viaggio tra arte, architettura e cinema [Journey Through Art, Architecture and Cinema]*. Monza: Johan & Levi, 2015.

16 Preta, Lorena. *Geographies of Psychoanalysis*. Milan: Mimesis International, 2015.

17 "A South wind—has a pathos," in *The Poems of Emily Dickinson: Variorum Edition*, edited by Ralph W. Franklin, Cambridge, MA: The Belknap Press of Harvard University Press, Copyright © 1998 by the President and Fellows of Harvard College. Copyright © 1951, 1955 by the President and Fellows of Harvard College. Copyright © renewed 1979, 1983 by the President and Fellows of Harvard College. Copyright © 1914, 1918, 1919, 1924, 1929, 1930, 1932, 1935, 1937, 1942 by Martha Dickinson Bianchi. Copyright © 1952, 1957, 1958, 1963, 1965 by Mary L. Hampson. Used by permission. All rights reserved.

18 Benjamin, Walter. *Infanzia berlinese intorno al millenovecento [Berlin Childhood Around 1900]*. Italian translation. Turin: Einaudi, 2001, p. 18.

19 Phillips, Adam. *On Balance*. New York: Farrar, Straus and Giroux, 2010.

20 "The Wind took up the Northern Things," in *The Poems of Emily Dickinson: Variorum Edition*, edited by Ralph W. Franklin, Cambridge, MA: The Belknap Press of Harvard University Press, Copyright © 1998 by the President and Fellows of Harvard College. Copyright © 1951, 1955 by the President and Fellows of Harvard College. Copyright © renewed 1979, 1983 by the President and Fellows of Harvard College. Copyright © 1914, 1918, 1919, 1924, 1929, 1930, 1932, 1935, 1937, 1942 by Martha Dickinson Bianchi. Copyright © 1952, 1957, 1958, 1963, 1965 by Mary L. Hampson. Used by permission. All rights reserved.

21 Clément, Gilles. *Manifesto del Terzo paesaggio [Manifesto of the Third Landscape]*. Italian translation. Macerata: Quodlibet, 2005.

22 Settis, Salvatore. *Architettura e democrazia. Paesaggio, città, diritti civili [Architecture and Democracy. Landscape, Cities, Civil Rights]*. Turin: Einaudi, 2017, p. 71.

23 Andrea Zanzotto, interviewed by Pasolini, in *Poesie e prose scelte [Selected Poems and Prose]*. Milan: Mondadori, 1999, p. 106.

24 Franzen, Jonathan. "Postcards from East Africa," in *The End of the End of the Earth: Essays*. New York: Farrar, Straus and Giroux, 2018.

25 Augé, Marc. *Non-Places: An Introduction to Supermodernity*. London: Verso, 1998.

26 Foucault, Michel. "Eterotopie [Heterotopia]," in *Archivio Foucault 3. Interventi, colloqui, interviste [Foucault Archive 3. Interventions, Talks, Interviews]*. Italian translation. Milan: Feltrinelli, 1998, pp. 307–315.

27 Foucault, Michel. *Le parole e le cose. Un'archeologia delle scienze umane [The Order of Things: An Archaeology of the Human Sciences]*. Italian translation. Milan: Rizzoli, 2004, pp. 7–8.

28 Castells, Manuel. *The Internet Galaxy*. Oxford: Oxford University Press, 2001.

29 Hillman, James. *L'anima del mondo. Conversazione con Silvia Ronchey [The Soul of the World. Conversation with Silvia Ronchey]*. Milan: Rizzoli, 2001. Hillman, James. *L'anima del mondo e il pensiero del cuore [The Soul of the World and the Thought of the Heart]*. Milan: Adelphi, 2002. Hillman, James. *L'anima dei luoghi. Conversazione con Carlo Truppi. [The Soul of Places. Conversation with Carlo Truppi]*. Milan: Rizzoli, 2004.

30 Phillips, Adam. *On Balance*. New York: Farrar, Straus and Giroux, 2010.

31 Holub, Miroslav. "Brief Reflection on Maps," in *Poems Before and After: Collected English Translations*. Translated by Ian Milner. Hexham: Bloodaxe Books, 2006.

32 Agamben, Giorgio. "Intervista [Interview]," *Il manifesto—Alias*, September 9, 2006, pp. 1–5.

Chapter 13

Invisible landscape

Beauty be not caused It Is
Chase it, and it ceases
Chase it not, and it abides
Overtake the Creases

In the Meadow when the Wind
Runs his fingers thro' it
Deity will see to it
That You never do it

Emily Dickinson, no. 516[1]

In a posthumous book are Walter Benjamin's articles and reporting, from the 1920s, about distant places where the German philosopher had lived in childhood or had visited later on, as an adult. Claudio Magris reminds us that Borges, in one of one of his most famous books, *The Maker*, tells of a man who sets out to draw the world, and collects images of mountains, islands, bays, provinces, mansions, stars, and vessels—only to discover, as he nears death, that this labyrinth of landscapes actually portrays his own face.[2] It's a clear analogy to the places recounted by Benjamin. Inner space comes into contact with, and evokes, outer space. The past becomes present. Two immense spaces—memory and landscape—touch.

The theme of nostalgia is inseparable from the theme of landscape, because nostalgia is how memory inhabits time in space. The aesthetics of melancholy uses the landscape as a great cape for wrapping and

DOI: 10.4324/9781003252979-13

enveloping the objects of memory and imagination. Νόστος and ἄλγος, return and sorrow. Nostalgia is the desire to return to the intact place of origin—if it were to exist. "Nostalgia" entered the European vocabulary in the 17th century thanks to a Swiss doctor, Johannes Hofer, who was struggling with a widespread pathology among his compatriots who were forced to spend long stretches far from the mountains and valleys of their home. "Nostalgia" became the term for this *mal du pays* or *Heimweh* (literally "pain of the house"). Nostalgia is the link with a lost landscape, a landscape that we no longer possess. A vivid mourning. Nostalgia is even gratitude toward the power of memory and imagination that deludes us into thinking we can find it again. Nostalgia, ultimately, is a form of evocative landscape. The place we seek, the landscape we select as our *querencia* (to use the term for the spot in the bullring where the bull feels safe) is inevitably permeated with nostalgia. (The bull, after all, senses the fate that awaits him.)

"The beauty of a landscape resides in its melancholy." With this epigram, Orhan Pamuk invites us to read *Istanbul*, the book he wrote for his city.[3] In the chapter called "Sadness" he tells us about old black and white photos of Istanbul that capture that particular melancholy known in Turkish as *hüzün*, "this feeling that the city of Istanbul carries as its fate."

Hüzün is different from simple sadness. While its meaning is linked to pain and missing, on one hand, it does also on the other hand lead us into a sacred zone, a poetic zone, in some ways akin to the idea of the Romantic notion of the sublime. Pamuk's sadness is not, therefore, a personal feeling that an individual gets in a certain circumstance, but the very essence of the city, permeated with a feeling that both defines its essence and structures that of its inhabitants. The person who lacks *hüzün* is the one who suffers; the person who has *hüzün* does not. It makes me think of Calvino's invisible cities. Istanbul is like Calvino's Zenobia, which prompted the author to muse that some cities erase desires or are erased by desires—while other cities are shaped by the desires of the inhabitants.[4]

Each of us begins life with islands of unexpressed potential that will become a Self. Perhaps when we immerse ourselves in a landscape—or lose ourselves in the streets of a city—we leave the Self free to return to its potential, to dialogue invisibly with evocative objects from our past, to float on Bollas' swing. Something that was and no longer is;

something that could have been and has not been. Objects preserved as psychic states that we have not completely understood and that we discover again, unchanged, in recurrent aesthetics, waiting to be known afresh in forms of mental vitality.

> When you return after a long time to your country or to the city where you were born or the street where you lived as a child, you feel the weight and the resurfacing of memories and, with them, a certain joy that comes from the place. Usually we think that all this comes from our mind, that it comes from the brain, because that is what we have been taught. But it is the place that speaks of itself.[5]

Yes, places talk about themselves, but not out of animism. They speak through our brains, through our memories, our ties. Places are within us: in the occasional lights, in the fluctuating weather, in unexpected encounters, in ancient solitudes. Maybe that's why we photograph them: to be sure. That's why we suffer when we see that they've changed—as if they've betrayed us. They're so much ours that: "All the places I have seen, / that I have visited, / now I know—I am certain: / I have never been there."[6]

In silence, the space between us and the landscape becomes narrower. The external world offers us a form; we give it a memory.

It's an evening in August, the ferry is leaving the port. I go out on the bridge to look at the sea and the receding coastline, but I am soon forced below deck: outside, at deafening volume, is a nasty musical soundtrack, a bad soundscape. The mixtape in restaurants; loud TV in cafes; people having noisy phone conversations even in the expensive "quiet cars" on the train; jet skis roaring over the sea pulling rubber bananas loaded with swimmers. Noise has become obligatory: perhaps it fills the void for people who don't know what to say, and so it covers over enigmas and sounds of silence. I have deep sympathy for the acoustic ecologist Gordon Hempton and his cause: "defending silence." He began with a spot in the rainforest on the Hoh River, where he placed a red stone: his starting point to change the world. Our auditory horizon—how far off a sound we can hear—is nearly 30 kilometers away, in silent places. Defending this "square inch of silence," Hempton preserves, intact, almost three thousand square kilometers of the silence of nature, which—as we know—has its own voice. Noise pollution, like light pollution, breaks that silence and that penumbra in which, for centuries, we have tried to listen to nature and see our own face. *Silence! The thorn penetrates deeper into your heart: / it binds with the rose.*[7]

If *mindscape* is a neologism for evoking the visual encounter between psyche and landscape—for the places we seek in the world to give a form and a solidity to something that is already within us—we could perhaps use the term *soundscape* for what gives acoustic form to our mental states. For the sounds that we find in ourselves as we discover them in the world. Canadian composer R. Murray Schafer launched the theory that soundscapes make up our acoustic world.

Oliver Sacks's *Musicophilia* begins with a story from a science fiction novel by Arthur C. Clarke. In this story, the aliens—who are intelligent but insensitive to music—devote themselves to studying us humans without understanding why we spend so much time listening to, performing, and composing music, something so evanescent and so useless. If the spaceship had landed among the Kaluli of Papua New Guinea, perhaps the aliens would have gotten better clues, because—as Steven Feld reports in his astonishing treatise, *Sound and Sentiment: Birds, Weeping, Poetics, and Song in Kaluli Expression*—the Kaluli rework nature's sound streams and bird song modulations with music. From there comes the experience-feeling of sound communication. Although some rare humans do, like those aliens, perhaps lack the neural apparatus to appreciate sounds or melodies, music still does wield enormous power over most people. It excites and depresses; it gilds our memories and scratches at old wounds; it irritates and amuses. I cannot listen to the aria about the tangled knot from Rossini's *Cenerentola* without laughing, for example. Chopin's preludes move me because they entered my soundscape in my childhood when my mother played them on the piano. And any time I hear Mina singing "Città vuota," I am swamped with nostalgia and admiration. (You've heard this song too: in *Godfather III*, in the Disney/Pixar movie *Luca*, and in numerous advertisements. It's a song of yearning that speaks to many people; to me, it brings nostalgia for my adolescence and admiration for the vocal revolution that Mina embodied for my country.)

Because of the extraordinary tenacity of musical memory, the soundscapes of childhood remain, Sacks says, "engraved in the brain." There is no music without the unconscious, and no unconscious without memory. William Styron, in *Darkness Visible: A Memoir of Madness*, reports that a piece of Brahms' Rhapsody for Alto saved him from suicide. Devoid as it is of "meaning," music neither conveys concepts nor formulates propositions, but works deep in the neuropsyche. It is a kind of writing that reaches the illiterate, a kind of vision that touches the blind; it triggers the imagination, plunges into memory, slips into solitude. And it carries a paradox: the same score that evokes pain also produces consolation. The denizens of soundscapes are sorted into infinite groupings: omnivorous musicophiles and sophisticated melomaniacs, introverted dodecaphonists and encyclopedic songwriters. And then there are the people who are allergic: "I can't listen to jazz," one obsessive patient tells me, "it has no contours; you don't know where it's going; that's why it distresses me." For Theodor Reik, the Austrian psychoanalyst who collaborated with Freud, the melodies that flow through the mind can provide an analyst with clues that lead to the secrets of a patient's emotional life, because the music that accompanies our conscious thought is never accidental.

Even when it is not playing—even when it merely accompanies us in a drowsy memory—music is healing. Scientific studies show that music promotes neurological and psychic repair work in our brains. Neuroimaging techniques clearly depict how listening to music can enhance neural connections in many brain regions. At the bedside of a comatose patient, relatives play recorded music to walk the patient back to the world by stepping in those audio footprints. Expectant mothers rest musical sources on their pregnant bellies: long before language blossoms, they will chant songs like primordial Kaluli music.

If the negative face (let's even say the Shadow, in the Jungian sense) of mindscapes are non-places (according to Marc Augé[8]), sometimes I think that our soundscapes are grazed by the shadow of non-musics. And it's precisely in the non-places that non-musics spread easily: sonic plastic, lounge music for waiting rooms and designer restaurants. What if vinyl was a re-appropriation of one's own soundscape?

As in the oceans and glaciers, there is wonder within silence, but also a kind of violence that can frighten us. Why fear? Perhaps because of feelings that we do not know how to accept; or because beauty has something unbearable about it. Something similar to Bion's O that, in its elusiveness, is revealed in the landscape. A truth without lies that needs the lie of the word to be expressed.[9]

Del Giudice in *Orizzonte mobile*, a novel/diary of his Antarctic expedition, writes:

> Despite the great violence, nature here is not hostile nor (even less so) friendly; it's just indifferent to the human presence that's a completely accidental fact. For us, the landscape is always a feeling of the landscape, but here what we call landscape does not spring from consciousness; rather it alters it and imposes another direction on it.[10]

It happens that it is not we who change the landscape (thanks to our possibilities of movement and the mobility of our gaze): it is the landscape that halts us. There is a moment when the ocean and the glacier, the desert and the plateau, get the upper hand on us. They transform us.

Letting oneself be transformed by the landscape opens up an "interior space," a space of "renunciation." Perhaps this is what Rilke means with the verses we considered near the start of this book: "For the existence of a tree to work for you, wrap around it some of the intimate space that dwells within you. Contain it on all sides. It is not delimited by itself. Only if you give it form will your renunciation become a true tree." "Renunciation," here, for Rilke, means opening up to one's surroundings. A relationship that is at once "detachment" and "closeness," intimacy and estrangement: psyche in the landscape and landscape in the psyche, in a single movement.[11]

The landscape is not only what we shoot photos of on a sunny day. Sure, there is a landscape that is welcoming, consoling. A landscape that's not only a place for our caretaking, but also a place that cures us. But there is also a landscape in need of our care and our attention; a *fragile landscape*—as it was beautifully defined by Antonella Tarpino—poised between past and future, between nature and memory; the emblem of a disoriented way of living, the emblem of a crisis in the practice of places. A landscape that shows its wounds, and—at the same time—invites us to attempt to suture shut those wounds. And, lastly, there is a landscape that inspires fear and attenuates our omnipotence: its indifference reduces us to silence. All three of these are expressions of our bond with places, which can contemplate the human and the inhuman, care and detachment, poetry and muted speech, silence and the unspeakable. Perhaps this, too, is what that *oh* (O?) is trying to tell us, in the line that Rilke wanted on his tombstone: "Rose, oh pure contradiction, joy of being no one's sleep under so many eyelids."[12]

All these are elements of that aesthetic conflict that, early on, dazzled our existence with the face-landscape that was the first to lean over and look at us—or did not know to look at us, or could not look at us.

In 1962, Heidegger traveled to Greece, in search, he said, "of the Greek element." He wondered, though, whether he would ever be able to "experience the initial Greek element," or if this experience would be predetermined, and therefore limited, by the present horizon. He feared that "every effort to reach the beginning remains vain and ineffective, even when, albeit within certain limits, there is some outcome."

Where is the landscape? The landscape is invisible within us. It is like the island of Delos: the Manifest, the Evident. Which was, for Heidegger, "she who, unconcealed, unveils; but who, at the same time, conceals and protects... Delos, the sacred island, the center of Greece, of its coasts and of its seas: it makes manifest the very instant in which it conceals." It was because of the experience at Delos, said Heidegger, that his trip to Greece became a stay in Greece: "Pure disclosure—in itself concealed—of the mountains and the islands, of the sky and the sea, of plants and animals."[13]

How, then, can I stay in the landscape? I understood something about how to do this when I sat with a great writer of the American Renaissance, Nathaniel Hawthorne:

> the best way to get a vivid impression and feeling of a landscape is to sit down before it and read, or become otherwise absorbed in thought; for then, when our eyes happen to be attracted to the landscape, you seem to catch Nature at unawares, and see her before she has time to change her aspect. The effect lasts but for a single instant, and passes away almost as soon as you are conscious of it; but it is real for that moment. It is as if you could overhear and understand what the trees are whispering to one another; as if you caught a glimpse of a face unveiled, which veils itself from every willful glance. The mystery is revealed, and, after a breath or two, becomes just as much a mystery as before.[14]

The "landscape" is not only that portion of nature that shows itself to our eyes. It is the invisible place in which the external world and the psychic world meet and mingle, inaugurating new boundaries. To see a landscape, we must have already "dreamed of" it. To touch it and be touched by it—as Emily Dickinson taught us—just a window is enough.

The landscape is our psyche in the world. We must listen to it and respect its capacity to sustain beauty, grace, and menace. Like a dream or like a poem, it has at least one spot that is unplumbable—a navel, as it were, that is its point of contact with the unknown.[15] In manifesting itself, it hides. So much so that, when we leave, we establish its advent.

Notes

1 "Beauty be not caused—It Is" in *The Poems of Emily Dickinson: Variorum Edition*, edited by Ralph W. Franklin, Cambridge, MA: The Belknap Press of Harvard University Press, Copyright © 1998 by the President and Fellows of Harvard College. Copyright © 1951, 1955 by the President and Fellows of Harvard College. Copyright © renewed 1979, 1983 by the President and Fellows of Harvard College. Copyright © 1914, 1918, 1919, 1924, 1929, 1930, 1932, 1935, 1937, 1942 by Martha Dickinson Bianchi. Copyright © 1952, 1957, 1958, 1963, 1965 by Mary L. Hampson. Used by permission. All rights reserved.

2 Borges, Jorge Luis. *L'artefice [The Maker]*. Italian translation. Milan: Adelphi, 1999, p. 197.

3 Pamuk, Orhan. *Istanbul: Memories and the City*. Translated by Maureen Freely. London: Faber & Faber, 2005. The opening line on melancholy is a quote from Ahmet Rasim.

4 Calvino, Italo. *Le città invisibili [Invisible Cities]*. Milan: Mondadori, 1972.

5 Hillman, James. *L'anima dei luoghi. Conversazione con Carlo Truppi [The Soul of Places. Conversation with Carlo Truppi]*. Milan: Rizzoli, 2004, p. 95.

6 Caproni, Giorgio. "Esperienza [Experience]." In *Il muro della terra [The Wall of the Earth]* (1964–1975). In *L'opera in versi [The Verse Works]*. Milan: Mondadori, 1998.

7 Celan, Paul. *Silenzio! [Silence!]* in *Papavero e memoria [Poppy and Memory]*. In *Poesie*. Italian translation. Milan: Mondadori, 1998.

8 Augé, Marc. *Non-Places: An Introduction to Supermodernity*. London: Verso, 1998.

9 See Chapter 1, Note 7.

10 Del Giudice, Daniele. *Orizzonte mobile [Mobile Horizon]*. Turin: Giulio Einaudi Editore, 2009.

11 Rilke, Rainer Maria. *Poesie sparse [Scattered Poems]* (n. 98), Italian translation in *Poesie [Poems]* (1908–1926), Vol. 2. Turin: Einaudi, 1995, p. 291.

12 Rilke, Rainer Maria. *Poesie [Poems] (1908–1926)*, Vol. 2. Turin: Einaudi, 1995.

13 Heidegger, Martin. *Soggiorni. Viaggio in Grecia. [Sojourns: The Journey to Greece]*. Italian translation. Parma: Guanda, 1997, pp. 39–40.

14 Hawthorne, Nathaniel. *Twenty Days with Julian and Little Bunny by Papa*. New York: New York Review of Books, 2003.

15 Freud, Sigmund. *The Interpretation of Dreams*, in *The Standard Edition of the Complete Psychological Works*, Vol. 1–24. London, The Hogarth Press and the Institute of Psychoanalysis, 1953–1974.

Chapter 14

Farewell

E ora che avevo cominciato
a capire il paesaggio:
"Si scende," dice il capotreno.
"È finito il viaggio."
Giorgio Caproni, "Cancellation"[1]

To respect the rhyme scheme, I would render this as: "And now that I have begun / the landscape to understand: / "Time to get off," the train conductor says. / "The journey is at its end."

Note

1 Caproni, Giorgio. "Disdetta [Cancellation]," from "Entremets [Entremets]," in *Il franco cacciatore [The Free Hunter]* © 2024, Garzanti S.r.l.p, Milan, Gruppo editoriale Mauri Spagnol.

DOI: 10.4324/9781003252979-14

For Product Safety Concerns and Information please contact our EU
representative GPSR@taylorandfrancis.com
Taylor & Francis Verlag GmbH, Kaufingerstraße 24, 80331 München, Germany

www.ingramcontent.com/pod-product-compliance
Lightning Source LLC
Chambersburg PA
CBHW070342270326
41926CB00017B/3942

9 781032 181257